Flea Market
Makeovers
for the
Outdoors

BJ Berti

Flea Market Makeovers for the Outdoors

Projects & Ideas Using
Flea Market Finds &
Recycled Bargain Buys

Bulfinch Press

New York • Boston

Bulfinch Press

Time Warner Book Group
1271 Avenue of the Americas
New York, NY 10020
Visit our Web site at www.bulfinchpress.com

First Edition

Library of Congress Cataloging-in-Publication Data

Berti, BJ
  Flea market makeovers for the outdoors : projects and ideas using flea market finds and recycled bargain buys / BJ Berti. — 1st ed.
      p. cm.
Includes index.
  ISBN 0-8212-2861-7
  1. Furniture — Repairing — Amateurs' manuals. 2. Used furniture. 3. Outdoor furniture. I. Title.
  TT199.B47523 2003
  749'.8 — dc22

                              2003020919

Design by Lisa Soraghan, Two of Cups Design Studio

PRINTED IN CHINA

Contents

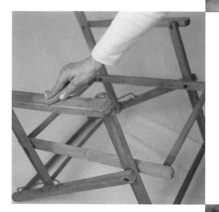

TO MY MOTHER, ELAINE, WITH LOVE

Acknowledgments

I am indebted to the following friends for generously allowing me the use of their various outdoor spaces as locations to photograph the projects in this book: Our neighbor Ann Bredahl; Dede and Joe Cummins; Annette Breindel; and my mother, Elaine Blumgart. Thanks to all for sharing with me.

Many thanks to George Ross for his terrific photographs, produced during the worst week of stormy weather of the summer, and to Cathryn Schwing for her invaluable help in making the photos look great.

Great thanks are due to my friend Stuart Klein for his many ideas, suggestions, and loans from his collections, and for his enthusiastic support of this project. Thanks also to John Hughes for his brilliant carpentry skills. To Vivian Cacia, my grateful thanks for your help with the right idea at the right time. And to Carson Cummins (and her parents, Joe and Dede) for agreeing to attend my tea party.

At Bulfinch, many thanks to Jill Cohen and Karen Murgolo for wanting to work with me and to Kristen Schilo, my editor, for making it happen so easily. Thanks also to Lisa Vaughn-Soraghan at Two of Cups Studio for her lovely and sensitive design.

To Denise McGann, again for her interest and support, thanks as always. To my son, Alex, many thanks for your help when we most needed it. And last but not least, I would like to acknowledge and thank my husband, Vincent Scilla, for all his contributions to this book from the excellent step-by-step photography to his hard work transforming the projects. It is not exaggerating to say I couldn't have done it without him!

Also many, many thanks to the following people and companies who supported this book through their contributions of various materials. Eileen Macomb at Benjamin Moore was very generous and helpful. Thanks for the paint! Marta Strekowski at Laura Ashley for Kravet supplied many of the lovely fabrics, and Dean Stadel at Mokuba helped out with fabulous ribbons and trims. Fairfield generously supplied many Soft Touch pillow inserts, and Oilcloth International supplied colorful oilcloth.

Introduction

YOU CAN TRANSFORM YOUR FAVORITE OUTDOOR LIVING spaces into useful and stylish areas for entertaining and relaxing using recycled and renovated flea market finds. This book demonstrates step-by-step how, with a little elbow grease and some ingenuity, you can turn cast-offs into charming and practical pieces to enhance your porch, deck, backyard, and garden.

In recent years, fixing up the porch and other outdoor areas in distinctive ways has become a key priority for homeowners. Using outdoor spaces for the things we love to do — be it eating a simple meal, visiting with family and friends, or just enjoying a nap in the fresh air — is an important addition or even a necessity in our hurried lives. Unfortunately, new furniture and accessories for the porch and lawn can be prohibitively priced, and less expensive pieces can often lack character. But lots of bargains, cast-offs, and other pieces of less than perfect furniture are waiting to be unearthed at flea markets, garage sales, and thrift stores. Home improvement stores and the big discount operations carry lots of simple, basic, inexpensive pieces that can also be enhanced and made more personal with a little thought and desire. Identifying these pieces is not difficult, and with imagination you can make them into useful and charming additions to your outdoor living areas.

At any yard sale or other secondhand spot, you can find metal or wicker furniture, odd chairs, benches, old shutters, small tables — even the makings of a birdbath or an outdoor candelabra — at rock-bottom prices. Take these "finds" home, roll up your sleeves, and the creative process begins! Clean the objects thoroughly, strip paint, remove rust, and add decorative design elements that turn ordinary items into objects that are uniquely yours.

As you set out to track down makeover-worthy flea market items, keep in mind a few basic "rules of the hunt." Don't overlook items that seem totally unusable: a rusty chair, a wicker table with an area in need of reweaving, or a shelf painted an ugly color. Take a chance on a less than perfect object and it is entirely possible for you to turn it into something that you can use and enjoy.

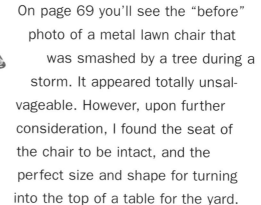

Also keep in mind that not every piece is worth salvaging. If a piece requires more work than would be justified by the end result, pass it by. Here are a few helpful rules I follow when sorting through flea market offerings:

- If an object is cheap enough and I can imagine how it might look once I've painted or otherwise refurbished it, I buy it, even if I don't have a specific need or place for it at that time.
- Pay attention to the object's overall shape and design; I won't buy something unless its shape is pleasing to me.
- Ignore the current color or fabric; if a piece has good bones it can usually be made to look good again.
- After you've finished looking, look again. Some of the best things I've acquired were things I had overlooked at first.
- Don't buy something that's really falling apart — unless it's a real bargain. In that case, take a chance. You can always throw it out later.

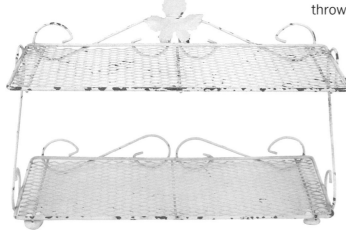

On page 69 you'll see the "before" photo of a metal lawn chair that was smashed by a tree during a storm. It appeared totally unsalvageable. However, upon further consideration, I found the seat of the chair to be intact, and the perfect size and shape for turning into the top of a table for the yard.

When your goal is to furnish outdoor rooms, certain things are always worth buying, assuming the price is right: wicker pieces; lawn furniture or smaller pieces in wood, iron, and metal; old lighting fixtures that can be transformed for candles; salvaged decorative metal fencing; trim; shutters; garden tools; and trellises.

Take some time before you hit the flea market to educate your eye to recognize good design. Look at shelter magazines that specialize in outdoor spaces and visit outdoor-furniture shops — the higher quality the better. Once you've done your homework, trust your instincts and work to develop your style. Be inspired by the things you love, experiment with color and pattern, and work toward a look that is truly your own. Have the vision to see beyond the apparent, and keep your eyes and imagination open as you shop.

Let chance guide you and be inspired by what the hunt turns up. Any object holds the promise of trans-formation, however unprepossessing it appears to start with, if treated with imagination. Use this book as a guide to inspire your creativity — you can use the projects as they are or as jumping-off points for your own ideas. Whatever approach you take, have fun transforming your flea market finds into lovely and unique pieces that will make any outdoor living space a marvelous place to entertain or to simply smell the roses.

Just remember: There is no such thing as a worthless piece of junk.

Porch and Deck

A NATURAL EXTENSION OF YOUR HOME, A porch or deck is the perfect place to create an outdoor living space that's distinctly your own. Whether it's a wraparound expanse on the front of your house, a screened-in area on the side, or a redwood deck in the backyard, a porch or deck can be turned into an inviting outdoor space that's perfect for relaxing, entertaining, or enjoying meals with your family. You can bring as much style to an outdoor space as you can to an indoor one. Take some time to think about what furniture and accessories you'll need to make it functional and comfortable — or leave it to chance and take your inspiration from what turns up.

When you're shopping, try to see beyond the obvious. For example, a pair of paneled-glass doors was the starting point for constructing the simple, stylish cabinet here. Exploring ways to further enhance the glass doors, I came upon a spray-on finish called Looking Glass used to create a mirrored effect on plain glass. Some brief experimentation with the spray led to the effect of antique-looking glass I wanted. Now the cabinet looks as if it has been around for ages — just the result I was hoping for. In addition, having extra storage space on the porch is very useful — a place to organize the games, extra candles, and other items that accumulate makes the porch feel more like a living space.

Folding screens have become very popular and are quite easy to construct from both new and old shutters, doors, or windows. Their flat surfaces are perfect places to try out a new decorative technique or effect. Make a stencil pattern by tracing a large-scale floral motif, as I

did. Or combine a few different floral motifs to make a new design. Use the photocopier to experiment with the scale of your design — try enlarging (as I did) or reducing the pattern before making your stencil. Alternatively, you can use a purchased stencil or make photocopies and decoupage them onto the screen.

A freestanding screen is a pretty and practical deck or porch accessory whether you use it to provide privacy for an outdoor shower, to create a cozy nook, or as a purely decorative accent.

Metal pieces in various states of rust pop up frequently at yard sales. You can leave them as they are (see Basic Techniques, page 151, for a way to preserve their natural state) or clean and paint them for a more polished look. The graceful half-moon-shaped table here was covered in rust when I acquired it. Getting rid of the rust was not too difficult, and

the results were well worth the effort. Used by the front door, it performs multiple functions — as a perfect serving table or buffet, or to hold seasonal displays of leaves or flowers.

Many smaller metal tables turn up at yard sales and flea markets, usually missing their original glass tops. You can simply replace the glass or take the opportunity to use the metal frame as a base for creating a new top. Used throughout the centuries from ancient to modern times, mosaic tiles are an ideal outdoor material, as they are both hard wearing and long lasting. Colorful, stylish, and easy to work with, they look good in any outdoor setting. As mosaic tiles are available in a wide range of colors, a tabletop can be made to enhance any decorating scheme. Suitable for beginners, a simple project like this one is an easy introduction to this enduring craft and results in a perfect addition to any porch.

Last, keep your eyes open for the larger attention-getting pieces of outdoor furniture like the hanging swing on page 22. Surely the pièce de résistance of any porch, a swing or its cousin, a glider, can be hard to find, but they are well worth tracking down. Wooden pieces like this swing are easily fixed up with paint, and new cushions, to soften the hard surfaces, can be made or bought. Sure to be a favorite spot for all, a swing can be the focal

point of your porch or deck — and the most popular spot for sitting or napping.

Gilded Lunette Table

GILDING IS REALLY NOT THAT COSTLY OR TIME-CONSUMING to do. The modern sizes used are effective and faster drying alternatives to the traditional materials. Imitation metal leaf — like the aluminum leaf used here — is a less expensive alternative to silver leaf. It looks quite nice, especially with the base coat of blue paint to complement and highlight the silvery tones of the leaf.

Originally, this table probably had a marble top, but an inexpensive and easily obtainable top can be cut from frosted glass.

1. Use steel wool or a power drill with wire brush attachment to grind as much of the loose rust and corrosion off the table's surface as you can. Use a wire brush to clean the corners and crevices that are hard to reach with the drill. [photo a]

2. If necessary, apply a product like Rust-Oleum Rust Reformer, following directions on the container. Then prime the table with a rust-preventive metal primer, following the instructions on the container. [photo b]

3. Sand the surface of the table lightly with fine-grade sandpaper or sanding sponge. Paint it with two coats of Cayman Blue paint. Let the paint dry completely between each coat and after the final coat.

4. Make a pattern for the tabletop: Place a large piece of paper or oaktag on the work surface. (Two or three sheets of drawing paper can be taped together if necessary.) Place the table top side down on the paper. Outline the tabletop with a sharp pencil. Have a piece of frosted glass cut to that shape at a local glass shop.

5 Gild the table's decorative embellishments, following the directions in the gilding kit. Pay special attention to applying the size. The layer of size should be flowed onto the area to be gilded very evenly and smoothly. It needs to be as even and as thin as possible so that all areas to be gilded will be ready at the same time. Apply only one coat and do not overbrush.

6 When the size has reached tack, apply the aluminum leaf, following the instructions in the gilding kit. Use a small pad of folded cheesecloth to press the leaf onto the surface. The pad will prevent the oils on your skin from discoloring the leaf and any fingerprints from being left on the surface. Make sure the cheesecloth does not touch the size. Brush away any excess leaf. [photo c]

7 Apply a thin coat of outdoor acrylic varnish to seal the gilded surfaces.

Materials

- Metal table
- Fine-grade steel wool
- Power drill with wire brush attachment
- Wire brush
- Rust-Oleum Rust Reformer and applicator
- Metal primer
- Fine-grade sandpaper (or sanding sponge)
- Benjamin Moore MoorGlo soft-gloss exterior paint in Cayman Blue 2060-50
- Disposable foam brush (or household paintbrush)
- Large sheet of paper or oaktag
- Pencil
- $1/2$-inch-thick frosted glass, cut to fit
- Basic gilding kit: gilding size, book of aluminum leaf, natural-hair brush, cheesecloth
- Outdoor acrylic varnish

Painted Porch Swing

THE PERFECT PERCH FOR A LAZY SUMMER DAY, A SLATTED-wood swing brings style and comfort to your porch. Changing the color from a bland, boring white to a lively green with blue accents, colors that look good in almost any outdoor setting, gives the swing a fresh, airy feel. A checked pillow adds to the retro look and softens the hard edges. When the project is completed, it is time to kick off your shoes and relax with a good book!

1. Sand the surface of the swing until smooth. If necessary, any uneven spots or cracks still remaining can be filled with wood putty.

2. Prime the entire swing with the acrylic primer. Sand lightly again. When the primer is dry, paint the flat slatted sections with two coats of Harrisburg Green paint. Let the paint dry completely between each coat and after the final coat. [photo a]

3. Paint the rolled back and bottom edges and the armrests with two coats of Freesia paint. Let each coat of paint dry completely. [photo b]

4. Screw in heavy-duty eye screws on the lower front and upper back of the outside of each armrest if they are missing. There should be holes to indicate where the eye screws are meant to go.

Materials

- Porch swing
- Power sander or sand-paper
- Putty knife
- Wood putty
- Disposable foam brush (or household paintbrush)
- Benjamin Moore Fresh Start acrylic primer
- Benjamin Moore MoorGlo soft-gloss exterior paint in Harrisburg HC-132 Green and Freesia 1432

- 4 heavy-duty eye screws
- 4 30-inch lengths of heavy-duty steel chain
- 6 heavy-duty quick-link connectors
- Tape measure
- Pencil
- Power drill
- 2 heavy-duty eye screws with attached hooks
- 2 34-inch lengths of heavy-duty steel chain
- 2 heavy-duty S hooks

5 Attach one of the lengths of 30-inch heavy-duty steel chain to the front eye screw on each armrest using a quick-link connector and feed the chain up through the hole in the top of each armrest. [photo c]

6 Attach a second length of 30-inch chain to each back eye screw using a quick-link connector. Hold the two chains on one side of the swing out so they meet and attach the chains at that point with a quick-link connector. Do the same on the other side. [photo d]

7 Hang the swing: Measure the distance between the two chains on each armrest. Measure and make a mark for each heavy-duty eye screw with attached hook on your porch ceiling, making sure the hooks will be inserted directly into a beam. With the power drill, make small starter holes, then screw the heavy-duty hooks into the ceiling beam. Insert the end loop of each 34-inch chain into each hook, add S hooks, and hook the chains attached to the swing to the S hooks. Adjust height if necessary.

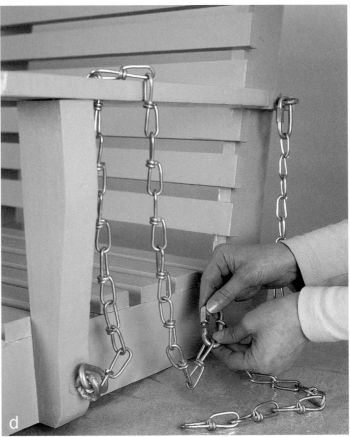

Mirrored-Glass Cabinet

EVERY PORCH CAN USE SOME STORAGE SPACE. HERE, vintage doors provided the starting point, and a local carpenter helped design and construct the cabinet. You can also pick up some new doors at the local home center. The Krylon Looking Glass Decorative Mirror-Like Paint used on alternating panes creates the illusion of aged glass, adding an interesting dimension to the cabinet front. The trick is to *not* clean the glass first; then when you spray the finish on, the unclean surface helps to create the mottled and clouded look of old glass.

① Remove all hardware and hinges from doors. Fill any holes with wood putty and sand if necessary.

② Measure your doors and adjust all the dimensions given in the materials list, if necessary, to fit the length and width of the doors you are using. Cut the wood using a circular saw to the sizes given in the materials list. Prime and paint all molding, knobs, legs, outside of sides, back, top, bottom, and doors with Caribbean Teal. Paint shelves, inside of sides, back, top, and doors with San Clemente Rose. (Alternatively, you could prime the pieces first, build the cabinet, and then finish painting it.)

③ Lay the two 63-inch cabinet sides flat, butted together, on the floor or a workbench. Mark "bottom" near one end of each board. Decide on shelf spacing; the shelves here are spaced to line up with the muntins of the doors. With a tape measure and pencil, make a mark on one board at each point where you want a shelf. For each point draw a line across both boards using the square and yardstick.

④ Mark the placement for the shelf screws: Measure and mark the center point along each line for a center screw, then measure and mark $1^1/2$ inches in from each end for two outside screws. With a drill and countersink bit, first drill a hole $^1/8$-inch deep on all marks, then switch to a drill bit and finish drilling all the marked holes for each shelf. The countersink holes will go on the outside of the cabinet frame. For ease in assembling later, on the insides of each board, make a chisel mark $^3/8$ inch below the row of holes — make a small mark at either end — to help line up the shelves.

⑤ From the 2x4 sheet of birch plywood, measure, mark, and cut a 13x36$^1/2$-inch piece for the bottom of the cabinet frame. Place the bottom piece on top of one of the shelves flush with the back edge and centered on the shelf from side to side. Screw the two pieces together from the underside with the $1^1/4$-inch screws. (The larger piece is the bottom of the cabinet and the smaller piece sits on top and is the bottom shelf.)

6 Mark the placement for the screws on the bottom and top pieces: Draw a line along all the outside short edges $3/4$ inch in from the edge. Measure and mark four holes starting $1^1/2$ inches in from the long edges, as you did for the shelves (step 3) on each short side of the top and bottom pieces. Predrill all the marked holes on the top and bottom pieces.

7 Position the metal plates for the legs on the underside of the bottom piece. Predrill holes for the mounting screws for the plates. Using a screwdriver bit, attach the plates to the underside of the bottom piece.

8 Assemble the outside of the cabinet as follows: Stand the cabinet sides up on end and fit the bottom piece in place with the smaller shelf piece on the inside and the bottom overlapping the sides. Fasten the bottom to the sides with $2^1/2$-inch screws in the predrilled holes. Set the top piece on top of the sides and fasten it to the sides with $2^1/2$-inch screws in the predrilled holes. Screw the legs into the metal plates on the bottom. [photo a]

9 Line up one shelf at a time with the chisel marks and fasten them to the sides with $2^1/2$-inch screws in the predrilled holes. [photo b]

10 Stand the piece on the legs and use a square and level to check that it is square. If it's not, bang on one corner to square up the frame. Lay the cabinet frame on the face of the lauan plywood, keeping the frame flush with the edges of the plywood. Draw a pencil line around the other two edges. With a circular saw, cut along those lines to make the cabinet back. Turn the cabinet frame onto its front and attach the back with 1-inch brads along the outside edges and along the shelves.

Materials

- Two multipaned glass doors (these are 62 inches long and $36^1/2$ inches wide)
- Two 63-inch $5/4$x12 pine boards for the cabinet sides (cut 1 inch longer than doors)
- Five 34-inch 1x12 pine boards for the shelves (cut equal to the width of the doors minus twice the thickness of one side) of the cabinet
- One $36^1/2$-inch 1x12 pine board for the top (cut to equal the full width of the doors)
- One $36^1/2$-inch $5/4$x$1^1/2$ pine strip for the top edge (cut to equal the width of the top piece)
- One 2x4-foot sheet of birch plywood $3/4$ inch thick for the cabinet bottom (cut to the same length as the top and the same width as the top, plus the thickness of the doors)
- One 4x6-foot sheet of lauan plywood $1/4$ inch thick for the cabinet back (cut to cover all the outside edges)
- 8-foot bed molding for the top edge
- 8-foot bullnose (or half-round) molding $1^1/2$ inches wide for the bottom edge
- Four metal plates for attaching the legs
- Four screw-in wooden legs $3^1/2$ inches high
- Four 3-inch butt hinges
- Two screw-in wooden knobs $1^1/4$ inches wide
- Forty-eight $2^1/2$-inch #8 wood screws
- Ten $1^1/4$-inch #8 wood screws
- 1 box of 1-inch brads
- 1 box $2^1/2$-inch finish nails
- Tape measure
- Pencil
- Square and yardstick
- Circular saw
- Miter box and saw
- Power drill with screwdriver, $3/8$-inch countersink bit, $3/16$-inch drill bit
- Small wood chisel
- Level
- Hammer
- Craft knife
- Paper
- Painter's tape
- Benjamin Moore Fresh Start acrylic primer
- Benjamin Moore Eggshell-Finish alkyd house paint in Caribbean Teal 2123-20 and San Clemente Rose AC-10
- Paint rollers, disposable liners, and tray
- Household paintbrush
- Krylon Looking Glass Decorative Mirror-Like Paint

⑪ Lay the butt hinges on the inside of the doors 5 inches down from the top and 10 inches up from the bottom. Mark the outline of each hinge by using a craft knife to score around all three sides of the hinge plate. This will keep the wood from splitting as you chisel out a mortise for the hinge plate to rest in. With the scored outline as your guide, chisel out just enough wood so the hinge can rest flush with the surface.

⑫ Predrill the holes for the mounting screws for the hinges. Install the hinges on the inside of each door. Hold the door on each cabinet frame, allowing a $3/16$-inch gap on the bottom for clearance (use shims or coins as spacers). Mark the outline of the hinges on the frame with a craft knife as in step 11. Remove the door and chisel mortises as in step 11. Hold the door in position again and predrill the holes for the mounting screws. Install the other side of the hinges on the cabinet frame. Do same with second door. [photo c]

13 With 2¹/₂-inch finish nails and a hammer, attach the 36¹/₂x1¹/₂-inch strip above the doors to the outside front of the top. The piece should be flush with the top and side edges.

14 Measure across the top front of the cabinet for the bed molding, and cut a piece to size using a miter box, mitering both ends. Measure and cut the side pieces to size, mitering the corners where the side molding meets the front molding and cutting the other ends straight. Attach molding to the top edge of the cabinet with 1-inch brads. Measure and cut the bullnose (or half-round) molding for the lower edge the same way as above. Attach it to the bottom edge of the cabinet with 2¹/₂-inch finish nails. [photo d]

15 Mark the placement of the wooden knobs for the doors and predrill holes. Insert screws and thread the knobs onto the screws.

16 Apply the Krylon Looking Glass paint to the glass panes: Cover alternating glass panes with paper cut to size. Tape around all the edges with painter's tape to hold the paper in place, covering all the wood surfaces. Also cover the outside wood frame with tape. Spray the unmasked glass panes with Looking Glass paint, following the directions on the container.

TIP: If you want the look of antique glass, do not clean the glass before applying Looking Glass paint.

Metal-and-Mosaic Table

A GOOD INTRODUCTION TO WORKING WITH MOSAICS, THIS small table with its colorful top is easily made and does not require a large investment in materials. The contrast between the hard-edged tiles and the fluid, graceful shape of the table's S curves and leaves contributes to its considerable charm. It is quite portable — easily transported to any part of your porch or garden that requires an extra surface. The lively colors and small scale add up to an accent piece that is both practical and attractive.

Materials

- Small metal table
- Sponge and bucket
- Household cleaner (like Soilex)
- Toothbrush
- Fine-grade steel wool
- Disposable foam brush (or household paintbrush)
- Benjamin Moore Fresh Start acrylic primer (optional)
- Benjamin Moore MoorGlo soft-gloss exterior paint in Blue Lagoon 2054-40
- Tape measure
- 1/2-inch marine plywood cut to fit opening in tabletop
- Exterior white glue
- Container for glue
- Glass mosaic tiles in 4 shades of blue and green
- Metallic mosaic tiles in assorted pale blue-green shades
- Palette knife
- Tile nippers
- Rubber or latex gloves
- Prepackaged grout in terra-cotta

❶ Wash the metal table frame with a soft sponge and lots of water with a cleaning agent like Soilex. Use an old toothbrush to clean in the corners and crevices that are hard to reach with the sponge. Rinse well and let it dry.

❷ Prepare the frame for painting by roughing up the surface lightly with fine-grade steel wool. If necessary, prime the frame with the acrylic primer. When the frame is dry, paint it with two coats of Blue Lagoon paint. Let it dry completely between each coat and after the final coat. [photo a]

❸ Using a tape measure, measure the opening on the top of the frame and have a piece of marine plywood cut to size. Dilute the exterior white glue with a small amount of water until it is spreadable and paint the plywood on top and all four edges with the glue-water mixture. Set it aside to dry.

❹ Plan the mosaic design by laying out the pieces of tile on the plywood until you are pleased with the pattern. Here I started with a border of three rows, constructed as follows: The outside row is a two-and-one alternating pattern of glass tiles in the darkest shades of blue. The next row alternates glass and metallic tiles both in similar shades of pale blue green that are much lighter than the outside row. [photo b]

❺ The third row repeats the lighter blue from the first row but alternates those tiles with a slightly different hue of medium blue. The overall effect of the three rows is that each row looks like a solid color, but the variations in tone and texture make for more interest. [photo c]

❻ The inside of the mosaic is an allover staggered 2x2 pattern in the two lighter shades of blue green. It is symmetrical, and some of the metallic tiles are used again in the very center. [photo d]

7 Glue the tiles into place using the exterior glue. Pour some glue into a small container and, using the palette knife, butter the back of each tile and stick it onto the surface. Let it dry.

8 Using the tile nippers, cut some tiles in half to make pieces for the outside edges as follows: Hold the tile firmly between your thumb and forefinger and apply pressure to the tile at the same time as you are pressing down on the nippers. This will help the tiles to snap cleanly in half. [photo e]

g

9 Glue these half tiles in place, as in step 7 above, on all edges, leaving bottom half of edge clear so top will fit in frame. Let it dry overnight. [photo f]

10 Wearing rubber gloves, apply the premixed grout following the directions on the package. Press the grout into the crevices between the tiles using your fingertips. Clean off the excess grout as recommended by the package directions. Let the grout dry overnight, then fit the mosaic top into the metal table frame. [photo g]

Stenciled Folding Screen

SCREENS CAN PLAY AS USEFUL A ROLE IN YOUR OUTDOOR living spaces as they do inside the home. They can help make an open, exposed space feel more private and contained. Old shutters like these, or newly purchased ones from the home stores, can easily be turned into a folding screen. The surface of the screen lends itself to traditional craft techniques like stenciling or decoupage, providing you with the opportunity to create an attractive one-of-a-kind decorative element. You can play with both pattern and scale, as this screen does, or color, to add a whimsical flourish to your outdoor decorating.

④ To stencil: Hold the stencil in place on one of the panels with repositionable spray adhesive and have the Rich Cream paint in a flat container nearby. Dip the stencil brush into the paint, but be careful not to overload it. Keep a paper towel nearby and tap the brush on the towel if you need to get rid of excess paint.

Gently dab the paint into the stencil with a pouncing motion. Try for allover distribution of paint across the surface but do not worry if it is not entirely even. Because my design runs over and onto the raised edges of the shutters, I had to hold the stencil down and push the paint into the corners. If you miss anything, you can fill it in afterward. [photos b and c]

① Sand the surface of the shutters until smooth. If necessary, any uneven spots or cracks still remaining can be filled with wood putty. Sand again after the putty dries.

② Prime the shutters with the acrylic primer. When the shutters are dry sand them lightly again and paint them with two coats of Bird's Egg paint. Let the paint dry completely between each coat and after the final coat.

③ To make your own stencil: Trace the image chosen onto a sheet of Mylar, acetate, or stencil card, or make a photocopy and stick the photocopied image right on top of the card or acetate with reposition-able spray adhesive. Cut out the image with a craft knife or a stencil cutter. (For this project, I worked with a photocopy of the pattern, which I traced onto a sheet of acetate using permanent marker, simplifying the design as I did so. The stencil was then cut using a stencil cutter.) [photo a]

TIP: When using permanent marker on Mylar or acetate, mistakes can be corrected by using alcohol and cotton swabs.

Materials

- 4 wooden shutters or panels
- Power sander or sandpaper
- Wood putty
- Putty knife
- Household paintbrush
- Benjamin Moore Fresh Start acrylic primer
- Benjamin Moore MoorLife flat exterior paint in Bird's Egg 2051-60 and MoorGard low-luster exterior paint in Rich Cream 2153-60
- Purchased stencil

- Repositionable spray adhesive
- Flat container for paint
- Stencil brush
- Small artist's brush
- Paper towels
- 6 bifold hinges
- Screwdriver
- Glides

Optional:
- Mylar, acetate, or stencil card
- Permanent marker
- Craft knife or stencil cutter

⑤ Allow the cream paint to dry, and add some small details, using Bird's Egg paint, to the design. [photo d]

⑥ Reposition the stencil on the panel and repeat the stencil instructions given in step 4. Here I staggered the pattern, stenciling the image twice on two of the panels and once on the other two panels. [photo e]

⑦ Small parts of the stencil can be used to add pattern to other parts of the panels if desired.

⑧ Hinge the panels together. You can add glides to the bottom of each panel if you would like to.

Glassware Candle Holders

LOADS OF GLASSWARE SIMILAR TO THE PIECES SHOWN here can be found at yard sales, flea markets, and thrift stores. Their weight and sturdy shapes make them perfect receptacles for the small tea lights that are sold in many stores. Generally, the cost of this type of glassware is so reasonable that you can splurge and buy as many different shapes and sizes as appeal to you. Clean them up with hot, soapy water and a little vinegar if necessary to remove any whitish film. Look for pieces in good condition and without scratches or chipped edges.

ⓐ Glassware and tea lights are waiting to be assembled. The insides of these small pedestal glasses are just the right size for the tea lights.

ⓑ If you want to see more of the candle flame, stack the tea lights on top of one another in deeper containers, like this fluted pressed-glass dish.

ⓒ A sturdy piece of restaurant glassware, originally a container for banana splits, now holds three tea lights in a row.

Materials

- Assorted sizes and shapes of glassware
- Tea lights

TIP: Add a small amount of water to the glass before putting the tea light in; it will make removing it and subsequent cleanup much easier.

Outdoor Entertaining

ONCE THE WARM WEATHER SETS IN, the backyard beckons for al fresco entertaining. There are so many possibilities: a picnic on the lawn, lemonade under a leafy tree, a child's tea party for a few special friends, a sunset celebration softly illuminated by candlelit chandelier, or an afternoon visit with a few good friends. Add your personal style to any outdoor entertaining event with flea market makeovers — use your imagination to envision the perfect setting for your makeovers and don't be limited to the obvious.

One of my favorite makeovers involved a large enough dose of imagination to see beyond the obvious and a bit more ingenuity and effort: turning the seat of a down-and-out metal lawn chair into an attractive tabletop. After detaching the seat from the rest of the chair, I removed many layers of old paint and applied a fresh coat of paint to the seat. I completed my makeover by constructing a wooden base to support the top, turning it into the perfect partner for an old Adirondack chair, freshly painted to match. You could look instead for legs rescued from an old wooden table — or even for new legs from a home building store — to use as a base. Look beyond the obvious for bases to support your top — any object that can support a flat piece can become a table base. And, of course, any flat surface can serve as a tabletop.

Seating is another essential for outdoor parties. If you entertain a lot, buy any folding chair, metal or wood, that appeals to you. You can never have too many comfortable outdoor seats. The small but sweet metal settee here needed only a good scrubbing and a coat of paint to revive it. New plump cushions in a glorious yellow fabric (weather resistant, of course) add to the comfort. When you find a special piece like this, you can build an entire outdoor room around it.

Every host or hostess also needs party helpers like trays and carryalls. Whatever kind of get-together you're planning, different shapes of trays are practical additions to all your entertaining. Plain metal serving trays, which you can pick up for a song at thrift stores, can be decorated in any number of ways, including with decoupage or by spraying with glossy paint. Decorations are optional but charming. Try to pick up any pieces that look salvageable; you never know when you might need them.

Wire baskets are another useful item for outdoor entertaining. Lined with checked oilcloth, they are great for organizing cutlery, glasses, plastic food containers, bottles, napkins, and other items for a picnic or an outdoor table.

Lighting creates the mood for any celebration indoors or out — extend your outdoor celebration into the evening with the imaginative use of lighting. Here a softly painted thrift store chandelier provides the illumination for a festive occasion. Turning old electric lamps and chandeliers into candelabras is an easy and fun makeover with dramatic results. Also look for interesting odd metal pieces, like gears or faucet handles, that can be used as holders for pillar candles or even mounted on a tree or wall as sconces.

Cushioned Love Seat

THERE ARE LOTS OF THESE TYPE OF METAL PIECES available at reasonable prices — sometimes you can find matching sets of chairs, love seats, and end tables. You can also collect them one by one as you find them. The smaller scale makes them easy to transport and quite suitable for smaller spaces like a terrace or deck.

This piece was in excellent condition, only needing a surface cleaning and an easy paint job to make it look presentable. Directions are included for making the cushions, but you can also opt to have them made by a local upholstery shop or seamstress.

Materials

- Metal-frame love seat
- Household cleaner (like Soilex)
- Sponge and bucket
- Toothbrush
- Fine-grade steel wool
- Disposable foam brush (or household paintbrush)
- Benjamin Moore Fresh Start acrylic primer (if necessary)
- Benjamin Moore MoorGard low-lustre exterior paint in Buxton Blue HC-149
- Tape measure
- Yardstick
- Permanent marker
- High-density foam, 5 inches in depth
- Craft knife or electric knife
- Polyester batting
- Spray adhesive for foam
- Pencil
- Clear plastic ruler
- Scissors
- Sun-resistant upholstery fabric
- Thread and 4 29-inch zippers to match fabric
- Sewing machine with zipper foot
- Pins
- Cotton cording for welting
- Household iron

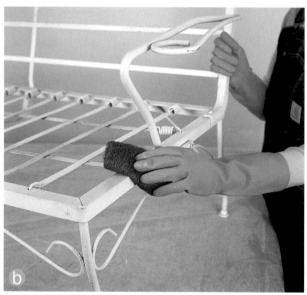

① Wash the metal frame with a soft sponge and lots of water with a cleaning agent like Soilex. Use an old toothbrush to clean in the corners and crevices that are hard to reach with the sponge. Rinse well and let it dry outdoors in the sun. [photo a]

② Prepare the frame for painting by roughing up the surface lightly with fine-grade steel wool. [photo b]

③ If necessary, prime the frame with the acrylic primer. (Here the existing surface was already painted a light color, so I did not need to prime.) When the primer is dry, paint the frame with two coats of Buxton Blue paint. Let it dry completely between each coat and after the final coat. [photo c]

④ Using a tape measure, measure the frame for the cushions. Here I wanted four cushions — two for the seat and two for the back. For the seat cushions, measure the depth of the seat and across the full width of the seat and divide the last number by two. When measuring for the back cushions, allow for the depth of the seat cushions when calculating the height. The width is the same as that of the seat cushions.

⑤ Cut the foam for the cushions as follows: With a yard-stick and permanent marker, measure and mark lines on the foam for each of the four cushions. If you have an electric knife, use it to cut the foam. Hold the knife parallel to the outside edge and cut straight down, like slicing through a loaf of bread, following the outline of the cushion. Or you can cut the foam using a craft knife. Cut very evenly in one smooth movement halfway through the foam, then cut the rest of the way through. Check the size by placing the cushions on the frame before continuing. [photo d]

⑥ Cover the foam cushions: Wrap the polyester batting around each foam cushion and trim it to fit, adding additional pieces of batting to cover the sides. With spray adhesive, attach the batting to each foam cushion and set aside.

⑦ Cut the cushion covers: Mark the measurements for the seat cushion on the fabric and mark a $1/2$-inch seam allowance all around the outside edges, using the plastic ruler to measure and marking as you go with the pencil. Cut out four pieces to these measurements from the fabric. Do the same for the back cushions, using those measurements.

To determine the length of the boxing strips, measure around the perimeter of the cushion form. The back boxing strip should wrap around the back corners of the cushion and extend onto the sides for 3 inches. Add 1 inch for seam allowances to the back piece. Make this piece 7 inches wide. Cut the front boxing strip to wrap around the front and sides of the cushion. Add 1 inch for seam allowance. Make this piece 6 inches wide. Split the back boxing strip in half lengthwise to insert the zipper and machine stitch it into place. Repeat for each cushion.

⑧ Cut enough $1^1/2$-inch-wide bias strips to use for welting on each set of back- and seat-cushion covers. Lay the cotton cord in the center of the wrong side of the bias strip and fold the strip in half, encasing the cord. Using a zipper foot, machine stitch as close to the cord as possible.

ⓓ

⑨ Assemble the cushion covers: With the right sides together and the cut edges aligned, pin the welting to the top of a cushion cover and machine baste it in place. With the right sides together, sew the assembled front boxing strip to the cushion top. Stop stitching about 2 inches before the end of the strip. With the right sides together, sew the back boxing strip to the cushion top. Stop stitching about 2 inches before the end. Seam together the front and back boxing strips. Fold the seams toward the front and finish attaching the boxing to the cover. Open the zipper 3 inches. With the right sides together and the cut edges aligned, pin the welting to the bottom cushion cover and machine baste it into place. With the right sides together, sew the bottom cushion cover to the boxing. Open the zipper and turn the cover right side out. Press if needed. Repeat for the other three covers. Insert the padded cushions into each cover.

Wire
Picnic
Baskets

VINTAGE METAL ACCESSORIES LIKE WIRE BASKETS, storage crates, small baskets, and buckets have a surprisingly contemporary flair because of their industrial materials. They also provide many creative possibilities for organizing and storage both inside and outside of the house. The wire baskets here can be used to transport all the necessities outside for a backyard picnic or they can easily go into the car for trips farther afield. The oilcloth liners are easy to clean and tie on for easy removal. The patina of the metal finish can be protected with a coating of linseed oil and a clear matte finish.

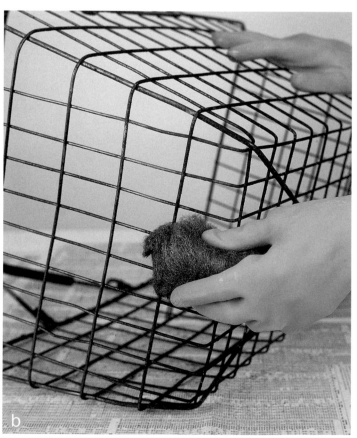

Materials

- Wire baskets
- Craft knife
- Rubber gloves
- Steel wool
- Tape measure
- Pencil
- Clear plastic ruler
- Drawing paper
- Masking tape
- Pins
- Scissors
- 2 yards each blue check and green check oilcloth

- White thread
- Sewing machine
- Pinking shears
- Fashion eyelets to match oilcloth
- Fashion eyelet tools
- Small hammer
- 4 yards each $1/4$-inch cord to match oilcloth

Optional:
- Small piece of mat board
- 1-inch-wide press-on hook-and-loop tape

① Remove any rubber from the basket handles using a craft knife and clean the basket with steel wool if necessary. If the finish is acceptable (the green basket here was nicely weathered and still had traces of original color), it can be left as is. [photos a and b]

② To make the liner pattern: With a tape measure, measure the basket's inside bottom length and width, then measure the depth of the basket. Draw a rectangle on paper equal to the same measurements as the bottom of the basket. Extend all the lines out to equal the same measurement as the depth of the basket and draw lines across at right angles to close the shapes. Tape sheets of paper together if necessary. You will have a pattern that is shaped roughly like a cross.

Cut the paper pattern out with the scissors and test the fit in the basket. Make any adjustments to the paper pattern needed. Make one pattern for each basket if they are different sizes.

③ Place the pattern on the oilcloth, tape or pin it into place, and cut out the shape with scissors. Repeat to make two shapes for each liner.

4 Pin two liner pieces together with the right sides facing out. Join them together by machine stitching around all the outside edges about $1/2$ inch in from the outside edge. With pinking shears, trim the edges about $1/4$ inch.

5 Mark the position of the eyelets, starting about $1^1/2$ inches in from the outside corners. You will need at least two on the short sides and four on the long sides depending on your basket. Place pieces of masking tape along the top edge of the liner approximately where the eyelets will fall. Use a clear plastic ruler to measure and mark the position of the eyelets on the pieces of masking tape, moving them if necessary. Following the directions on the package of eyelet tools, use scissors to make a starter hole before removing the tape, then remove the tape and insert an eyelet into the hole. Use the eyelet tool and a small hammer to attach the eyelets to the liner. [photo c]

6 Cut the cord into 12-inch lengths and insert into each eyelet. Tie a knot on each end of the cord as close to the end as possible. Trim if necessary. Insert the liner into the basket and tie it on.

7 Make an optional divider: Make a paper pattern to fit across the middle of the basket. (The one here measures 8 inches across at the bottom and 10 inches across at the top and is 7 inches high.) Trace the pattern onto a piece of mat board and cut it out with a craft knife. Check the fit in the basket — the mat board should fit the space loosely with room to move on each side. Using the board as a pattern, place it on the oilcloth and mark around the outside edges, adding 1 inch on each side and $1/2$ inch on the bottom and top edges. Cut out two pieces of oilcloth and sandwich the mat board between the two pieces with the right sides facing out, enclosing the board in the oilcloth. Make sure the board is centered and pin around the edges to hold it in place. Machine stitch around the shape as close to the edges of the board as possible — use a zipper foot to help you. With pinking shears, trim the edges about $1/4$ inch. Cut lengths of hook-and-loop tape to fit the side edges of the divider. Open a side seam and center the loop half of tape over the seam, press into place. Mark the position on the liner for the hook side of the tape and press it into place. Repeat for the other side of the basket. Insert divider into basket and press in place. [photo d]

Thrift Store Metal Trays

YOU CAN EASILY FIND PLENTY OF METAL TRAYS IN THRIFT stores and at yard sales. Many have seen better days and can be a little grungy, but they clean up very well. Look for interesting shapes and sizes. The heavier metal ones, like worn-out silver plate, are the sturdiest — if you can find them at a reasonable cost. But the shape is really what you are looking for. They can be decorated in any manner from decoupage to resist spraying or simply painted in different solid colors. They can add a touch of whimsy to any space and provide practical help ferrying things back and forth from indoors to out.

a

Materials

- Assorted metal trays
- Fine-grade steel wool
- Brown paper or drawing paper
- Pencil
- Scissors
- Spray paint in 2 contrasting colors (here ivory and pale green), 2 tonal colors (here peach and persimmon), 1 pale color (here yellow)
- Protective mask

- Repositional spray adhesive
- ³/4-inch round multipurpose labels
- Painter's tape
- Craft knife
- Purchased freeze-dried leaves
- Decoupage medium
- Small artist's brush
- Small foam brush (or household paintbrush)

① All trays: Clean the surface with steel wool, wash with dish soap and water, and dry carefully. [photo a]

② Ivory and green tray: Lay a piece of brown or drawing paper on the tray. Trace along the edges of the area you want to mask. Cut out the mask with scissors. Set it aside.

③ Spray the tray with two coats of ivory paint, following the directions on the can. Work outside or in a well-ventilated area and wear a protective mask. Let it dry.

④ Spray the edges of the paper mask with the repositional spray adhesive and position it on the tray, pressing the edges down firmly. [photo b]

⑤ Spray the unmasked edges of the tray with two coats of the pale green paint, as above. Let it dry. Remove the paper mask carefully. [photo c]

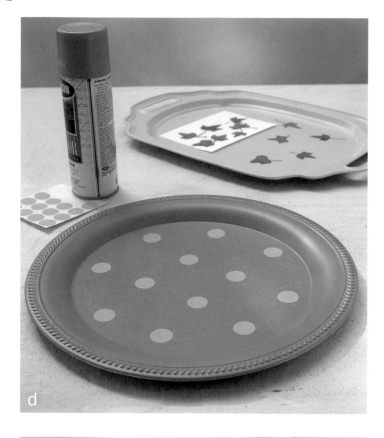

d

e

⑥ Polka-dot tray: Spray the tray with two coats of the peach paint and let it dry. Position the round labels on the tray as pictured and press the edges down firmly. With the painter's tape, mask the edge of the tray. Spray the tray with two coats of the persimmon paint, as above. Let it dry. [photo d]

⑦ Carefully remove the labels and painter's tape, using a craft knife to lift off the dots. [photo e]

⑧ Decoupage tray: Spray the tray with two coats of the pale yellow paint, as above. Let it dry. Position the freeze-dried leaves on the surface. Adhere the leaves to the tray by brushing the back of each one with the decoupage medium, using the small artist's brush. Press the leaves firmly and carefully into place, making sure all the edges and stems are sticking to the tray. When the adhesive is dry, coat the entire top surface of the tray, including the leaves, with the decoupage medium using the foam brush. Let it dry completely and then coat it a second time. [photo f]

f

TIP: For even coverage when spray painting, move the can slowly across the object being painted. Continue over the outside edge of the object and then go slowly back in the other direction.

Painted Candelabra

YOU CAN EASILY CONVERT AN ELECTRIC CHANDELIER INTO an outdoor candelabra by removing the light sockets and the wiring from the piece. This is quite a bit easier and faster than rewiring it! The quick painted finish used here is an easy way to change the color while adding a nice texture and patina to the metal surface. The subtle color complements the hobnail-patterned milk glass center, and because the technique highlights the nooks and crannies on the chandelier, it creates the illusion of an aged piece. It is also an extremely durable finish.

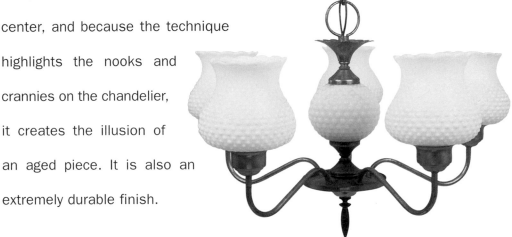

a

Materials

- Metal-and-glass chandelier
- Screwdriver
- Wire cutters
- Fine-grade steel wool
- Satin-finish spray paint in ivory
- 8 ounces Benjamin Moore Impervex high-gloss enamel in Stratton Blue HC-142
- 4 ounces acrylic glaze medium
- Container for mixing glaze coat
- Small foam brush (or household paintbrush)
- Paper towels

TIP: Use dripless candles in chandeliers or sconces. Wrap the ends of the candles with aluminum foil to make a snug fit if the holders are too large.

❶ Set aside the glass shades and take the chandelier apart in sections, keeping track of the sequence of parts so you can reassemble them later. If you have a digital camera, it can be helpful to take a "record" photo to refer to when reassembling the chandelier. Most of the pieces can be easily unscrewed to disassemble the chandelier. Set aside the central glass piece also.

❷ When you have exposed the wiring in the center section, use wire cutters to cut all the wires running out to each arm. You should be able to then pull out the wires running up through the central post. Discard the old wiring. Loosen and remove the screws holding the electric sockets in each arm. Remove the sockets with the attached wiring and discard them.

❸ Clean the metal sections of the chandelier with soap and water, if necessary, or with fine-grade steel wool. Spray them with two coats of the ivory spray paint. Let it dry for a few hours or overnight. [photo a]

4 Make the glaze coat by mixing 8 ounces of Stratton Blue paint and 4 ounces of acrylic glaze medium in a container. Add 4 ounces of water (a little at a time), stirring well. Working on one section of the chandelier at a time, apply the glaze thickly to the surface with the foam brush and let it dry for four to five minutes. [photo b]

5 Using a wadded-up paper towel, dab at the surface to remove most of the glaze, leaving a haze of color on the surface and a buildup of color in the details. Allow it to dry. Repeat until the desired level of color is achieved. Repeat with each section. [photo c]

6 When the painted pieces are dry, reassemble the lamp, setting aside the glass shades for the arms. Save them for another use or in case you should ever want to reassemble the whole chandelier.

Metal-Topped Side Table

A VERY LARGE TREE BRANCH CAME DOWN IN A STORM, smashing this lawn chair and collapsing the metal frame on itself but leaving intact the back and seat. Taking the sections apart to see if the seat or back could be salvaged, I discovered that although the back piece was very rusty, the seat was in good shape and could be recycled as a tabletop if I had a base to set it on. An existing Adirondack chair inspired the simple carpenter shape of the legs, and a very basic frame was constructed to connect them. Now the top (formerly the chair seat) fits snugly in place on the frame, held in place by the lip.

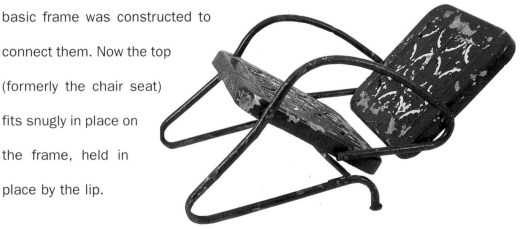

Materials

- Metal chair
- Vise grip
- Adjustable wrench
- Penetrating oil (like Gunk Liquid Wrench Super Lubricant) (if necessary)
- Old newspapers or plastic drop cloth
- Paint remover for metal
- 6-in-1 painter's tool
- Protective mask
- Protective eyewear
- Heavy-duty rubber gloves
- Stripping brush
- Soft rag
- Mineral spirits
- Disposable foam brush (or household paintbrush)
- Benjamin Moore Fresh Start acrylic primer
- Fine-grade sandpaper (or sanding sponge)
- Benjamin Moore MoorGard low-lustre exterior paint in Marlboro Blue HC-153
- One 10-foot $^5/_4$x10 pine board
- Tape measure
- Pencil
- Band saw (or scroll or jigsaw)
- Oaktag or thin cardboard
- Scissors
- Power drill with screwdriver and $^3/_{16}$-inch drill bit
- Level
- Square and yardstick
- 28 2-inch #8 wood screws

❶ Dismantle the chair by using a vise grip and an adjustable wrench to remove the bolts holding the seat to the frame. If the bolts are very rusty or hard to remove, use a product like Gunk Liquid Wrench to loosen them, following the directions on the container. Separate the seat from the frame and discard the frame or save it for another use. [photo a]

❷ Spread newspaper or a plastic drop cloth over your work area. Remove the paint from the chair seat with paint remover, following the directions on the container.

3 Scrape off the softened paint using the 6-in-1 painter's tool. Make sure to work outside or in a well-ventilated space and wear a protective mask, eyewear, gloves, and clothing. It might require many applications to remove all of the paint. Use a stripping brush to remove the last of the softened paint from hard-to-reach crevices. Remove any residue of the paint remover by wiping the piece with a rag dipped in mineral spirits. [photos b and c]

4 Once the metal is stripped, avoid letting it contact water, which can cause rust to form. Paint the seat with Fresh Start acrylic primer. Let it dry. Sand the surface of the seat lightly with a fine-grade sandpaper or sanding sponge. Paint it with two coats of Marlboro Blue paint. Let it dry completely between each coat and after the final coat.

5 Measure and mark a 2-inch-wide strip down one side of the pine board. Divide the strip into two lengths measuring $13^5/8$ inches long and two lengths measuring $16^3/4$ inches long. These measurements will need to be adjusted to fit the inside dimensions of your top. Cut the four 2-inch-wide strips from the board using the saw.

71

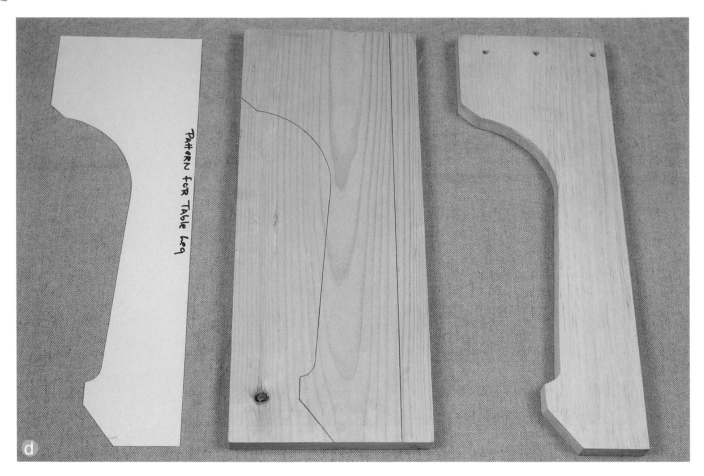

6 Enlarge the pattern for the table leg (or make your own). Trace the pattern on oaktag or on a piece of thin cardboard. Cut out the pattern with scissors. With pencil and pattern, trace four table legs on the remaining length of pine board. Cut the legs out using the saw. [photo d]

7 Assemble the frame as follows: Predrill two holes on each end of the shorter frame pieces about $1/2$ inch in from edge. On a flat work surface, stand one shorter piece on edge and butt one of the longer frame pieces against the shorter piece (use a level and square to check that the corners are square and the frame pieces level) and fasten them together with screws in the predrilled holes. Butt the other longer piece against the same shorter piece and fasten as noted above. Butt the other shorter piece against the two longer pieces and fasten as above to complete the frame.

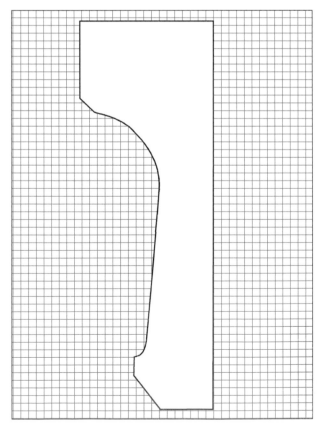

Enlarge pattern for leg 570% (height should measure $20^{5}/8$") or adjust for desired height.

8 Predrill three evenly spaced holes across the top edge of each leg about $^3/_4$ inch down from the top edge. Place the preassembled frame on a flat work surface and line one leg up with the outside longer edge of the frame. Fasten the leg to the frame with the screws in the predrilled holes. Repeat for all four legs. For additional stability, add two more screws across the top of each leg from inside the frame. [photo e]

9 Paint the frame with Fresh Start acrylic primer. Let it dry. Sand the surface of the frame lightly with fine-grade sandpaper or sanding sponge. Paint it with two coats of Marlboro Blue paint. Let it dry completely between each coat and after the final coat. Set the top in place on the frame. [photo f]

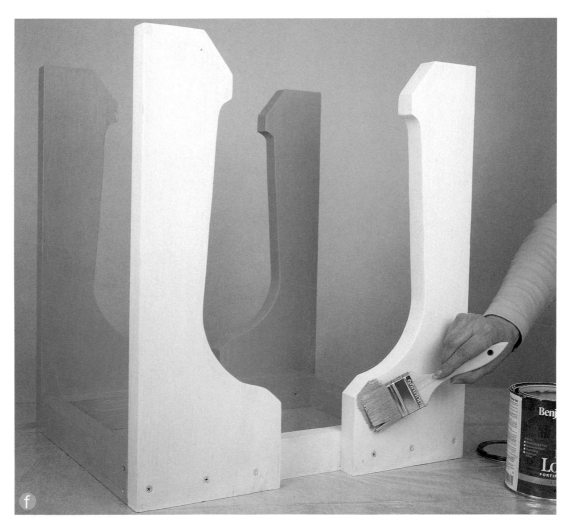

Child's Rocking Chair

A FRIEND BOUGHT THIS SMALL-SCALE METAL ROCKING chair for her daughter but had not gotten around to fixing it up. She was delighted when I offered to fix it up — and I was pleased to have the chance to make something enjoyable for a young girl. The cottagey floral print on the cushion seemed just the right scale for this chair. Rather than go for the obvious and paint the chair pink, I chose a soft green that nicely sets off the colors in the fabric. The back of the chair looked a little bare and in need of some softening. The easy-to-make pop-over top fit the bill — and the ties add extra interest to the top of the chair as well.

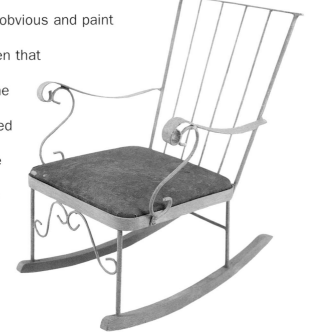

Materials

- Child's chair
- Screwdriver
- Pliers
- Permanent marker
- 1/2-inch-thick foam
- Craft knife
- Scissors
- Polyester batting
- Staple gun and staples
- Floral fabric
- Clear plastic ruler
- Soft lead pencil or water-soluble fabric marker
- Tape measure
- Pins

- Thread
- Sewing machine
- Household iron
- Spray starch
- Fine-grade sandpaper (or sanding sponge)
- Disposable foam brush (or household paintbrush)
- Benjamin Moore Fresh Start acrylic primer (if necessary)
- Benjamin Moore MoorGard low-lustre exterior paint in Palisades Park 439

1 Remove the screws holding the seat to the chair and set the screws aside until later. If the seat is not screwed in, remove it by pushing up on it from underneath.

2 With the pliers and screwdriver, remove the staples or tacks holding the seat cover in place and remove the old cover. Using the screwdriver, lift up the center of each staple and twist so one end is loose. Pull the loosened staples out with the pliers. Discard old foam or stuffing used for seat. Set the old cover aside to use as a pattern. [photo a]

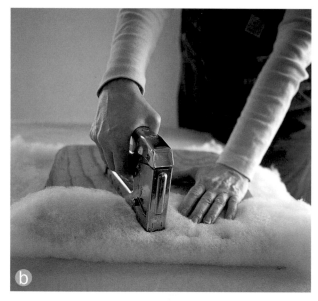

3 Using the wooden seat base as a pattern, trace the outline on the foam with the permanent marker. Trim the foam to fit the base using a craft knife. Cut out new padding from the polyester batting, again using the base as a pattern, allowing 3 to 4 inches extra all around for wrapping around the base. Place foam on base and wrap the batting around the foam and base and staple it in place, stretching it tightly over the wooden base as you go. Start stapling the batting to the base with a staple in the middle of two opposite sides, and then do the same on the other two opposite sides, spacing staples about 1/2 inch apart. Continue to staple on either side of the centers, alternating opposite sides, pulling the batting tight. When you reach a corner, fold the batting diagonally across the corner and place one staple in the corner to hold the batting. Fold the sides in neatly and staple them into place. After you have completed stapling the batting, it can be trimmed close to the staples. [photo b]

4 Using the old cover as a pattern, cut a new one out of the floral fabric, centering the pattern if necessary, adding 4 to 5 inches extra all around. Staple the fabric in place over the batting in exactly the same fashion as above and trim the fabric close to the staples when finished. [photo c]

5 Measure across the widest part of the top of the chair and as far down as desired for the popover top. Double the length and add 4 inches to that measurement. Add 3 inches to the width. Cut a piece from the floral fabric for the top, using these measurements, and centering the pattern if necessary. Cut four strips of fabric 2 inches wide and 20 inches long for the ties.

6 Assemble the top: Fold the ties in half the long way with the right sides together and pin together down the long side, allowing a $1/2$-inch seam allowance. Machine stitch down the long edge and across the bottom edge. Trim the seam allowance, turn the tie inside out, and press. Repeat for the others.

On larger piece of fabric fold bottom edges up $1/2$ inch and then $1^1/2$ inches to make bottom hems. Pin in place and machine stitch across both hems. Fold side edges in $1/2$ inch and then 1 inch. Before stitching side edges, insert a tie to the depth of the bottom hem into each outer corner so they hang down below the edge. Pin in place. Pin the side edges in place and machine stitch. Stitch across the ties along the bottom edge and the top edge of the ties to hold them in place. Press using spray starch. [photo d]

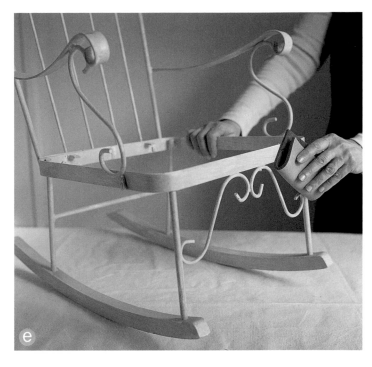

7 Sand the surface of the chair lightly with fine-grade sandpaper or sanding sponge. If necessary, prime the chair with an acrylic primer. When it is dry, sand it lightly again and paint with two coats of Palisades Park paint. Let it dry completely between each coat and after the final coat. [photos e and f]

Vintage Floral Picnic Cloth

SCRAPS OF TWO NEW PRINTED FLORAL FABRICS ARE combined with pieces of a smaller-scale vintage printed chintz to make this picnic cloth. The faded patterns of the prints, both new and old, are set off by a central square, in a similar weight, of creamy off-white vintage linen. Generally, old printed cottons look best when mixed with other cottons, either new or old, that are similar in tone, weight, and texture. The wide rickrack trim is a particular favorite of mine — it is used here to outline the different sections of the cloth, separating each of the fabrics and uniting the whole.

1 Use a clear plastic ruler and a pencil to measure and mark four squares measuring $11^3/4 \times 11^3/4$ inches on the smaller piece of floral fabric. Cut the squares out using scissors and set them aside.

As above, measure and mark two rectangles each measuring $19 \times 11^3/4$ inches on one of the larger scraps of floral fabric. Cut the rectangles out and set them aside.

Measure and mark two rectangles each measuring $21 \times 11^3/4$ inches on the other larger scrap of floral fabric. Cut the rectangles out and set them aside.

Measure and mark one rectangle measuring 19×21 inches on the off-white fabric. Cut out the rectangle and set it aside. [photo a]

M a t e r i a l s

- About $2/3$ yard each of 2 different floral fabrics
- About $1/3$ yard of third floral fabric
- 19×21-inch piece of off-white linen or cotton
- Pencil

- Clear plastic ruler
- Scissors
- Pins
- Sewing machine
- Household iron
- Thread to match fabrics
- $4^1/2$ yards 1-inch-wide off-white rickrack

2 Lay each row out as shown, with the smaller squares in the corners and the off-white piece in the center. Working across the top row, place the side edge of each piece on top of the next piece, allowing the edges to overlap $1/2$ inch on each side. Pin the pieces together. Sew the first two pieces together using a zigzag stitch, machine stitching down the center of the overlapped seam (see photo b). Join the third piece to the first two. Set the top row aside. Join the next two rows, as above, until all three rows are completed. Next, join the rows to one another in the same manner as above. Press the completed cloth.

3 Finish the cloth by making a mitered hem as follows: Place the cloth right-side down on an ironing board or padded work surface. Using the clear plastic ruler as a guide, fold the cut edge of the fabric up $3/4$ inch. Press the fold to form a crease. Repeat until $3/4$ inch has been pressed up on all four sides.

Following the directions above, fold the pressed edge up an additional 2 inches. Press the new fold to form a second crease parallel to the first. Repeat until the additional 2-inch crease has been pressed up on all four sides. Unfold the second crease. [photo b]

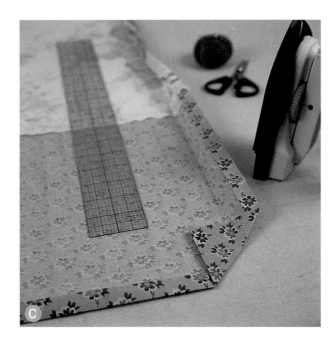

4 Keeping the fabric right-side down, use the clear plastic ruler to mark a diagonal line across each corner at the intersection of the inner crease lines. Fold each corner up toward the center along that line and press the corner into place. [photo c]

5 Fold the pressed 2-inch hem up again, re-pressing the crease lines, and iron each corner flat, enclosing the pressed corner fabric to form a miter. If it is too bulky, the fabric can be trimmed by cutting across the corner about $1/2$ inch from the folded edge before folding up the hem again. Pin the hem in place and edge stitch along the folded edge. If necessary, hand stitch the mitered edges together. [photo d]

6 Measure and cut two lengths of rickrack to fit across the width and two lengths to fit down the length of the cloth. Add 1 inch to each piece for turning the ends under. Pin the rickrack in place, covering the zigzag stitching on the seams. With the sewing machine, straight stitch through the middle of the rickrack while turning the ends under to finish. Pin and stitch the two vertical lengths first, then the two horizontal strips. [photo e]

Lawn and Garden

HOW WOULD YOU DESCRIBE THE PERFECT OUTDOOR room? Maybe it's that quiet area of your yard you can retreat to at the end of the day, gathering your thoughts as you relax on a comfortable chair. Perhaps it's a shaded wicker chair where you can practice your newest hobby. Or, possibly, the perfect outdoor room might simply be the spot closest to your garden, where you can take in the fragrance and beauty of the flowers through the seasons from a pretty garden bench.

The possibilities for creating outdoor rooms that you'll love living in are as far-reaching as your imagination. And decorating these spaces with flea market makeovers will enable you to achieve exactly the look you want. Set the stage for comfort and express your individuality; be inspired by what you see here or look for other intriguing objects to express your personality.

Serving as a focal point in even the simplest of gardens, benches come in wood, metal, and many other materials, and in styles ranging from rustic to ornate. Many classic designs in wrought iron or steel are available — even the simplest style can serve a useful function in designing an outdoor space. Look for interesting shapes like that of the bench here, with the simple, elegant curves — even covered in rust this bench looked stylish! I added a cushion in a floral green-and-white fabric to coordinate with the soft green color of the bench.

When I first saw the wood-and-canvas lawn chair at a tag sale, complete with an attached footrest below and a canopy frame overhead, I thought how great it would be to stretch out in and unwind. It needed a new canopy cover, and I added a matching cushion for the footrest. Because the existing fabric was practically in shreds, I re-covered the entire chair. It wasn't difficult. Instead of the classic stripes, I chose a new (and weather-resistant) polka-dot fabric that, even though it is modern, has all the appeal and charm of vintage. Don't get stuck thinking that everything has to be vintage or flea markety; sometimes a modern element is just what a piece or a room needs to make it really special. I'm convinced that the chair looks better now than when it was brand-new!

You'll always be able to find wicker pieces, in various states of disrepair, at any secondhand venue, whether it's a garage sale or an estate sale. As long as the repairs are minimal — a coat of paint, simple reweaving — seen-better-days wicker is a terrific buy. The two most available pieces are tables and chairs. If they are cheap enough, by all means, buy them. Easy to paint, they blend in well with almost any decorating style, depending on what color and fabric you choose. White has become the traditional color for wicker, but black can look very fresh, especially paired with cushions or pillows in a classic mattress-ticking fabric. Bright colors are dramatic and fun, and they can work well in both traditional and modern settings. A scratched top on a wicker table can easily be camouflaged with decoupage — or perhaps a mosaic top made from shards of thrift shop china if you are more ambitious.

Wooden folding chairs are another frequent flea market find — and a sensible purchase for any additional seating you might need. These chairs are practical and portable, but they're also plain. You can easily spruce them up with paint in a solid color or a simple, long-lasting decorative paint effect. You can also add tie-on seat cushions or simple-to-sew, easy-fitting slipcovers.

From the woolen throw fashioned from old sweaters to the wicker table decoupaged with flowers to the graceful garden bench, use the projects in this chapter to inspire you to turn your lawn and garden into an outdoor space of charm, grace, and comfort.

Curved Iron Bench

THIS LOVELY METAL BENCH WITH A CURVED BACK HAD certainly seen better days when I rescued it from my friend Stuart's deck. It had been left outside for many years and was almost entirely covered in rust. A little work with a power drill and wire brush got rid of the worst areas, then I treated it with Rust-Oleum Rust Reformer, a product that chemically converts rust into a smooth, paintable surface so there's no need to sand to bare metal. The oblong pillow in a tonal floral pattern adds an extra touch of luxury and comfort.

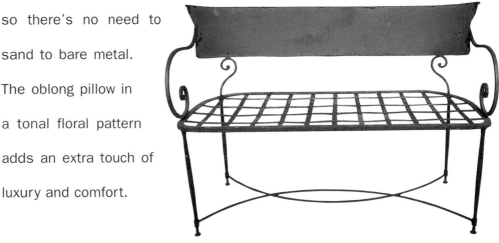

Materials

- Metal bench
- Power drill with wire brush attachment
- Wire brush
- Rust-Oleum Rust Reformer and applicator
- Rust-preventive metal primer

- Fine-grade sandpaper (or sanding sponge)
- Benjamin Moore Impervex high-gloss enamel exterior paint in Stratton Blue HC-142
- Disposable foam brush (or household paintbrush)

❶ Use a power drill with wire brush attachment to grind as much of the loose rust and corrosion off the surface of the bench as you can. Use a wire brush to clean in the corners and crevices that are hard to reach with the drill. [photo a]

❷ If necessary, apply a product like Rust-Oleum Rust Reformer, following the directions on the container. Prime the bench with a rust-preventive metal primer, following the directions on the container. [photo b]

a

③ Sand the surface of the bench lightly with fine-grade sandpaper or sanding sponge. Paint the bench with two coats of Stratton Blue paint. Let the paint dry completely between each coat and after the final coat.

TIP: Rust-Oleum Rust Reformer chemically converts rust into a smooth, paintable surface, so there's no need to sand to bare metal. It is compatible with most paints.

Painted Wicker Chair

DID YOU KNOW THAT *WICKER* CAN REFER TO MANY different materials such as bamboo, paper, rattan, or other natural fibers that are bent and woven into pieces of furniture? If you find a natural unpainted piece of antique wicker, rub a little linseed oil into the surface to restore it to its natural glory. Painting it will decrease its value. But an old chair like the one here can be easily painted without worry. Wicker looks good in bright colors, and a few structural flaws can be covered up with plump pillows and paint. It's been used for outdoor furniture since the Victorian era, and for good reason — it is durable and very comfortable on hot, sticky days.

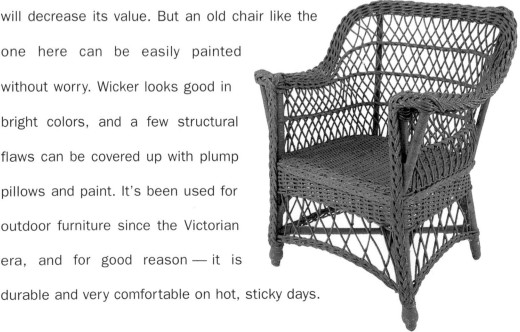

1. Wash the wicker chair with a soft sponge and lots of water with a cleaning agent like Soilex. Use an old toothbrush to clean in the corners and crevices that are hard to reach with the sponge. Rinse well and let it dry outdoors in the sun. [photo a]

2. If necessary, prime the chair with the acrylic primer. (For this project, I was painting a dark color and the existing paint was in reasonable shape, so I did not need to prime.) When it is dry, paint it with two coats of Plum Perfect exterior paint. Let it dry completely between each coat and after the final coat. [photo b]

3 Make the pattern for the seat cushion: Place a piece of paper on the chair seat or deck. Outline the edges with a soft lead pencil. Remove the paper pattern and draw a vertical line down its center with ruler and pencil. Fold the pattern in half along that line, with the traced outline facing out. Working on one half, straighten out the lines. Leave the paper folded in half and cut around the new line with scissors. Unfold the pattern and lay it on the chair seat to check the fit, making any necessary adjustments to the shape. Trace the outline of the paper pattern on a piece of oaktag to make a more durable pattern.

4 Cut the foam cushion: Lay the oaktag pattern on top of the foam. With the permanent marker, trace the outline of the cushion. [photo c]

Materials

- Wicker chair
- Sponge and bucket
- Household cleaner (like Soilex)
- Toothbrush
- Household paintbrush
- Benjamin Moore Fresh Start acrylic primer (if necessary)
- Benjamin Moore MoorGlo soft-gloss exterior paint in Plum Perfect 1371
- Paper
- Soft lead pencil
- Clear plastic ruler
- Scissors
- Oaktag
- Permanent marker
- High-density foam, 4-inch depth
- Craft knife or electric knife
- 2 yards floral fabric
- Pins
- 22-inch zipper to match fabric
- Thread to match fabric
- Sewing machine with zipper foot
- Cotton cording for welting
- Polyester batting
- Spray adhesive for foam

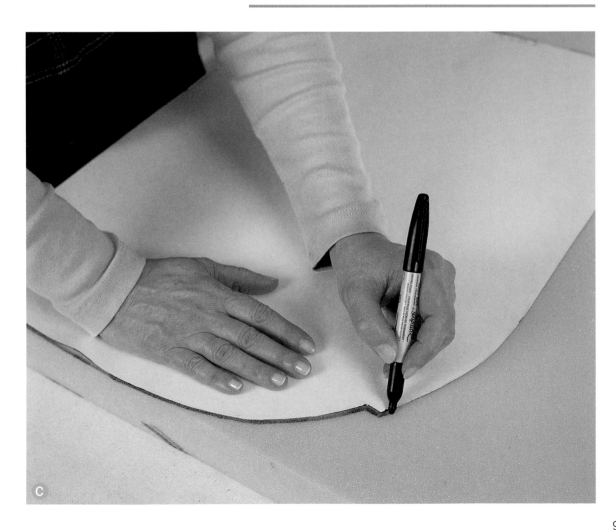

c

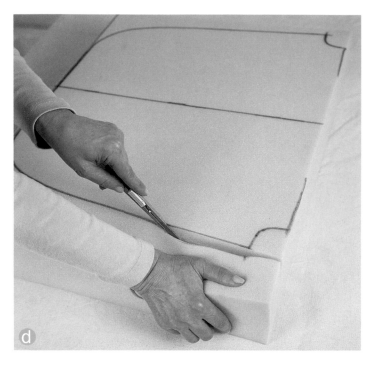

5 If you have an electric knife, use it to cut the cushion shape out of the foam. Hold the knife parallel to the outside edge and cut straight down, like slicing through a loaf of bread, following the outline of the cushion, or cut the foam using a craft knife. Cut very evenly in one smooth movement halfway through the foam, then cut the rest of the way through. [photo d]

6 Cut the cushion cover: Lay the cushion pattern on the fabric and mark a 1/2-inch seam allowance all around the outside edges, using the plastic ruler to measure and marking as you go with a pencil. Mark and cut out top and bottom cushion covers from the fabric. [photo e]

⑦ To determine the length of the boxing strip, measure around the perimeter of the cushion form. The back section should wrap around the back corners and extend onto the sides for 3 inches. Add 1 inch for seam allowances to the back piece. Make this piece 6 inches wide. Cut the front boxing strip, matching the floral pattern, to fit the front of the cushion. Add 1 inch for seam allowances. Cut two side boxing pieces to fit the sides of the cushion. Add 1 inch for seam allowances. Make these two pieces 5 inches wide. (Normally the boxing would be two pieces only, but because I needed to match the pattern, here it is in four pieces.) Split the back boxing in half lengthwise to insert the zipper and machine stitch it into place.

⑧ Cut enough $1^1/2$-inch bias strips to use for welting on the top and bottom cushion covers. Lay the cotton cord in the center of the wrong side of the bias strip and fold the strip in half, encasing the cord. Using a zipper foot, machine stitch as close to the cord as possible.

⑨ Assemble the cushion cover: Fit the boxing strips around the foam cushion and pin the seams together where they meet. Mark the seams and machine stitch the front and side boxing strips together. With the right sides together and the cut edges aligned, pin the welting to the top cushion cover and machine baste it into place. With the right sides together, sew the assembled front and side boxing strips to the top cushion cover. Stop stitching about 2 inches before the end of the strip. With the right sides together, sew the back boxing strip to the top cushion cover. Stop stitching about 2 inches before the end. Seam together the front and back boxing strips. Fold the seams toward the front and finish attaching the boxing to the cover. Open the zipper 3 inches. With the right sides together and the cut edges aligned, pin the welting to the bottom cushion cover and machine baste it into place. With the right sides together, sew the bottom cushion cover to the boxing. Open the zipper and turn the cover right side out. Press if needed. [photo f]

⑩ Cover the foam cushion: Wrap the polyester batting around the foam shape and trim it to fit, adding additional pieces of batting to cover the sides. With spray adhesive, attach the batting to the foam cushion. Insert the cushion into the cover.

Polka-dot Lawn Chair

WELL WORN BUT STILL USABLE WHEN I BOUGHT IT, THIS folding chair needed new canvas for the seat and back and was totally missing the fabric canopy. Luckily, it still had its matching footrest — frequently these are missing by the time these chairs turn up at flea markets. Refinishing the frame is easy. It is a little more time consuming to make the new fabric pieces, but they are simple to construct, as they only require straight-sewn hems on the side edges. The amusing lime green polka-dot sun-resistant fabric is a change from the usual awning stripes these chairs generally sport and is the perfect color for any outdoor setting.

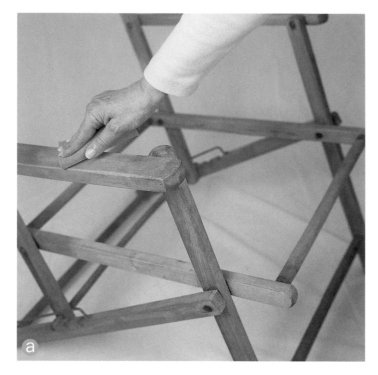

① Carefully remove the old fabric from the chair. Label each piece using a permanent marker and set them aside; these will be your pattern pieces.

② Sand the frame lightly with fine-grade sandpaper or sanding sponge. (If necessary, remove any finish first with paint remover or furniture refinisher.) [photo a]

③ Apply tung oil with a soft rag or cheesecloth, following the directions on the container. Repeat as needed until you have achieved the desired finish. Set the frame aside and let it dry completely. [photo b]

Materials

- Folding lawn chair
- Permanent marker
- Fine-grade sandpaper (or sanding sponge)
- Satin-finish tung oil
- Soft rag or cheesecloth
- Sun-resistant outdoor fabric
- Pencil
- Clear plastic ruler
- Tape measure

- Scissors
- Pins
- Household iron
- Thread to match fabric
- Sewing machine
- Ribbon trim or bias edging
- $1/2$-inch-thick foam
- Hand sewing needle
- Staple gun and staples
- Small hammer
- Brass upholstery tacks

④ Use the original three fabric pieces as patterns for the chair seat and back. Lay the old pieces out on the sun-resistant outdoor fabric, centering the pattern carefully. Use a pencil and ruler to mark all cutting lines on the fabric. Add $1\frac{1}{2}$ inches extra to all of the long sides for turning back and hemming. Add 3 inches extra to the top and bottom edges for wrapping and stapling the fabric pieces to the frame. If the edges will show, as they do on the upper back-rest section here, add an additional inch to each end so the raw edges can be turned under and hidden before tacking. (If the original fabric is missing, just measure the length and width where the fabric seat, back, or canopy will go, adding additional for hems and wrapping as above, or seam allowances if needed.) [photo c]

⑤ Cut out the seat pieces along the drawn lines. Turn the long sides under $1/2$ inch and then $1/2$ inch again, pin, and machine stitch into place. Press the hems carefully with an iron. [photo d]

⑥ Cut the fabric for the canopy. (In this case, I had to work from measurements, as the original was missing: Measure the length and width of the frame and add 2 inches to each measurement.) Turn the fabric wrong side up and bring each corner together to form a right angle seam, pin, and machine stitch together to form the canopy. Trim the excess fabric from the corner seams and press. Cover the raw edge with ribbon trim or bias edging and stitch.

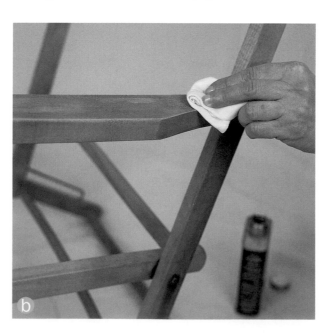

7 Cut one piece of fabric for the footrest cushion. (Again, take measurements if the original is missing: Measure the length and width of the footrest, then double the width and add 1 inch to each measurement for seam allowances.) Cut four pieces of ribbon trim 24 inches long for ties. Fold the fabric piece in half the short way, right sides facing in, pin a $1/2$-inch seam, and machine stitch. Press the seam open and center the seam in the middle of the back. Position the ribbon ties along the inside of the top edge seam allowance, making sure the ties fall to the inside. Pin a $1/2$-inch seam and machine stitch. Trim the fabric at the corners, turn it right side out, and press. Cut the foam to size and insert into the cover. Pin the seam closed along the lower edge. Hand sew it closed.

8 Wrap the fabric piece over the bottom seat frame and staple it into place. Wrap the chair back around the posts and turn the raw edges under. Hammer decorative brass upholstery tacks to hold the back in place, setting them about 1 inch apart. Staple the long piece into place, wrapping the excess around the frame, and trim if necessary. Fit the canopy top into place over the frame and tie on the footrest cushion. [photo e]

Metal Folding Chairs

ONE OF THE CHAIRS HERE TURNED UP AT A NEIGHBOR'S
yard sale and the other was found by my husband at the local dump.
Both have sturdy metal frames and wooden seats. The green chair was
missing a few slats, but a local carpenter easily crafted new ones to
fit — duplicating the cutout detail in the existing back slat in one for
the seat. Two replacement pieces for the side edges of the red chair
were cut from scraps of wood lattice and hammered into place. Both
chairs lend themselves to simple paint treatments — this
one is easy, fast, and useful. The final glaze coat
mutes the colors and, when scrubbed away, reveals
the layers beneath to leave a multi-
tonal surface. This creates a
more complex and richer surface than
flat, single-color paint on its own.

Materials

- Metal-and-wood chairs
- Paint remover
- Paint scraper
- Protective mask
- Wood putty
- Heavy-duty rubber gloves
- Power sander or sandpaper
- Putty knife
- Wood scraps for replacement slats and side pieces (if needed)
- Hammer and nails
- Household paintbrush
- Benjamin Moore Fresh Start acrylic primer

- Benjamin Moore MoorGlo soft gloss exterior paint in the following colors:
  Pink Begonia 2078-50
  Paradise Pink 2078-40
  Grape Green 2027-40
  Stem Green 2029-40
- Glazing medium
- Artist's pigment craft paint (like Plaid's FolkArt) in the following colors:
  White
  Burnt Sienna
  Hauser Green Light
- Small containers
- Synthetic steel wool

❶ Remove the old paint from the metal frame and wood slats or seat of the chair with paint remover, following the directions on the container. Scrape off the softened paint using the paint scraper. Be sure to work outside or in a well-ventilated space and wear a protective mask, gloves, and clothing. [photo a]

❷ After removing the paint, sand the surfaces with the power sander or sandpaper. Fill any uneven spots with wood putty and sand again, if necessary. Replace any missing pieces, if necessary. Then prime the chair with Fresh Start acrylic primer. Let it dry. Sand it lightly again. [photo b]

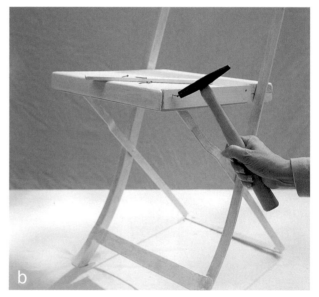

❸ For the rose chair: Paint alternating slats with Pink Begonia and Paradise Pink exterior paint. Paint the frame with the darker color (Paradise Pink). Let it dry completely.

❹ Make a glaze coat by mixing 4 ounces of glazing medium with 6 tablespoons of White craft paint, 4 tablespoons of Burnt Sienna craft paint, and 2 tablespoons of Pink Begonia exterior paint in a small container. Apply the glaze to the chair and let it dry. [photo c]

5 Scrub over the surface of the chair with the synthetic steel wool, lightly at first, to reveal some of the undercoat without taking off all of the glaze coat. Strive for an allover gently textured look. If you want more of the underlayer to show through, go back and scrub the surface again. Repeat the process until the desired effect is achieved. [photo d]

6 For the green chair: Paint the whole chair with one coat of Grape Green exterior paint. Let it dry completely and then paint the whole chair with one coat of Stem Green exterior paint. Let it dry completely.

7 Make a glaze coat by mixing 4 ounces of glazing medium with 6 tablespoons of White craft paint and 4 tablespoons of Hauser Green Light craft paint in a small container. Apply the glaze to the chair and let it dry. Repeat step 5 above, scrubbing the surface to reveal some of both underlayers of green paint. [photo e]

Decoupage Wicker Table

THIS WICKER TABLE LOOKS ENTIRELY DIFFERENT WITH ITS
coat of fresh cream paint and artfully scattered country garden
flowers — quite a change from its previous dingy mustard and dark
green colors. The top surface is still a little uneven — the idea was not
to make it perfect — but fresh and pretty. I would not suggest leaving
it outdoors in bad weather, but coating the whole top
surface with two layers of the
decoupage medium after adhering
the flowers makes the table surprisingly
durable. It should hold up well with many
years of use. The small woven detail in
the wicker base of the top is highlighted
with the same lavender paint used on
the wicker chair on page 90.

Materials

- Wicker table
- Fine-grade sandpaper (or sanding sponge)
- Putty knife
- Wood putty
- Household iron
- Iron-on wood-veneer edging
- Craft knife
- Household paintbrush
- Benjamin Moore Fresh Start acrylic primer
- Benjamin Moore MoorGlo low-lustre exterior paint in Rich Cream 2153-60 and Plum Perfect 1371
- Die-cut flowers and leaves
- Small square artist's paint-brush
- Decoupage medium
- Disposable foam brush
- Extra-fine-grade steel wool

❶ Sand the tabletop until it is smooth. If necessary, any uneven spots or cracks still remaining can be filled with wood putty. Using a household iron, iron the wood-veneer edging onto the outside rim of the tabletop. Any excess can be trimmed off afterward using a craft knife. Sand the veneer edging lightly and the tabletop again, if necessary. [photo a]

❷ Prime the entire table with the acrylic primer. Sand it lightly again. When it is dry, paint it with two coats of Rich Cream exterior paint. Let the paint dry completely between coats and after the final coat.

a

3 Punch out and arrange the die-cut flowers and leaves in a pleasing pattern on the tabletop. Brush the back of each flower and leaf with the decoupage medium using the small artist's brush. Press the flowers and leaves firmly and carefully into place, making sure all the edges are sticking to the tabletop. [photo b]

4 When the adhesive is dry, coat the entire surface of the tabletop, including the die-cuts, with the decoupage medium using the foam brush. Let it dry completely and apply a second coat. When it is dry, lightly go over the top with extra-fine-grade steel wool.

5 If desired, paint the woven wicker detail on the tabletop base with Plum Perfect exterior paint. [photo c]

Felted Patchwork Throw

THE RECYCLING OF WOOLEN FABRICS IS NOTHING NEW.
Old or new woolen sweaters, especially if they are boiled and felted —
either by design or by accident — are suitable for cutting up into
squares or other shapes and joined to make a patchwork throw or
blanket. Thrift stores hold racks of sweaters in a large range of colors
that are perfect for this purpose. Even raiding your or your friends'
closets can turn up a suitable woolen garment past its prime. Here the
luxury of the velvet and pleated-satin
trims contrasts with the under-
stated smoothness of the
knitted squares, adding a
touch of extravagance
and playfulness to this
small throw.

Materials

- 4 or 5 wool sweaters
- Scissors
- Household iron
- Heavyweight mat board
- Rotary cutter
- Self-healing mat
- Pencil
- Clear plastic ruler
- Pins
- Thread to match background color and trim
- Sewing machine
- Purchased binding
- Optional trims

❶ Turn the sweaters inside out and cut each sweater apart along the seam lines. Leave the ribbing on the lower edge of the body and sleeves intact. Starting at the lower edge of one side seam, cut up the side seam of the sweater and down the sleeve seam. Do the same on the opposite side seam. Cut as close to the seam lines as possible. Open the sweater flat, then cut around the sleeve seams to detach the sleeves from the body. Cut the neck ribbing off and then cut through the shoulder seams on each side. You will have four pieces from each sweater. Set the neck ribbing aside or discard it. With an iron, steam-press each section flat.

❷ Make a template out of the heavyweight mat board — the one used here is 6 inches square. Use the template, rotary cutter, and self-healing mat to cut squares from the sweater sections. Plan the squares to take advantage of any patterns the pieces might have. You can use the lower edging or ribbing if it is not too wide, otherwise it is better to cut squares from the other parts. [photo a]

❸ Arrange the squares in a pleasing pattern, moving them around until you are satisfied with the color placement. This one has eight rows of seven blocks. Once you have decided on your design, make stacks of the rows starting with the lower row. Stack the blocks with the first square you pick up on the top and finish with the last square on the bottom. Pin a piece of paper with the row number — 1, 2, etc. — on it to the top square in each stack as you finish the row. [photo b]

c

4 To assemble the throw, work on one row (one stack) at a time. Take the top square in a row and pin it to the next square with right sides facing, and machine stitch to join them. Take the next square and join it to the first two, and continue in this fashion until the whole row is joined together. Be careful to follow the stacked sequence. You will have a strip of seven blocks stitched together. Machine stitch each square to the next one using a zigzag or overlock stitch if your sewing machine has one. Keep the paper label pinned to the first square in each row. When all the rows are completed, steam press each seam as flat as possible.

5 Pin the first row to the second row with right sides facing, matching the seams as you pin across the row. Machine stitch the rows together. Continue until you have joined all the rows together. Steam-press again along the seams, pressing as flat as possible. [photo c]

6 Apply purchased binding to the outside edge. Add additional trims if desired. [photo d]

TIP: Use a washing machine to felt old wool sweaters if you can't find any at the thrift stores. Set the machine cycle for hot wash and small load. Place the sweater in a small mesh bag and throw it in the washing machine. Add a small amount of detergent and run through the wash cycle. Then either rinse the item by hand (to prevent further felting) or run it through one gentle rinse cycle. Let it spin briefly in the washer to remove any excess water. If you rinse by hand, put the sweater back in the machine to spin briefly. Lay the sweater flat to dry.

d

Flowers and Birds

A WIDE VARIETY OF FOUND OBJECTS CAN
be turned into containers or planters to suit any
outdoor situation. Metal and wooden pieces
can add age and character to your
garden — look for objects that have already
been ripened by the elements. Easy-to-find
and usually very reasonably priced galvanized metal buckets are a particular
favorite of mine for flowering plants. Find
them at flea markets or yard sales — or even
at your local recycling station. Frequently they
are discarded after developing a hole in the
bottom; just punch a few more holes for
drainage and fill them with geraniums or other
vibrant-colored flowers. Use different sizes of
tubs with a variety of plants for a more dramatic
effect. Watering cans, old wheelbarrows, feed
tubs, even old aluminum or enameled cook-
ware can be turned into terrific planters as
well. And every now and then, you might run
across an old farm implement or garden tool
that you can transform.

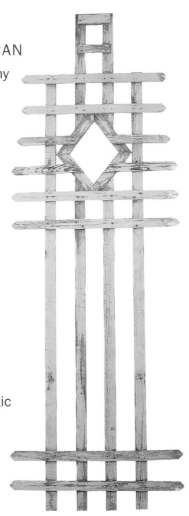

Adding a mirror to your garden is an old trick employed to fool the eye
and create the illusion of depth. Look for opportunities to incorporate a
mirror into your garden. It could be as simple as hanging a mirror on
your porch to reflect a wonderful view or layering an old mirror on a
fence to create the impression of a larger garden. With its rustic
finish and art deco–like design, a trellis like the one in this
chapter is enhanced by the addition of a small
mirror in the diamond shape at its center.
The intertwining strips of wood form a
perfect frame for a mirror. I like to look
for places like these where mirrors
can be incorporated. They are
easy to add and can be
a dramatic
enhancement to a

special — or not so special — object, especially outdoors, where their use is unexpected.

Instead of a wreath to decorate the front door, hang a metal flower holder filled with a seasonal bouquet. Used by florists, holders like the one here pop up now and then at flea markets. Share the beauty of your garden with your friends and neighbors. In summer, hydrangeas and snapdragons mix well together; in early fall, fill container with sunflowers, Queen Anne's lace, and a few brightly colored flowers like zinnias; in winter, sprigs of fragrant evergreens and red berries can hold up to the cold weather. It's a nice way to display flowers from your garden.

A birdbath or a small fountain is a pleasing addition to any garden. Many flea market finds can be used to improvise a simple fountain, and no backyard can be bird friendly without a birdbath, of course. Unmatched pieces are the starting point for the decorative and functional birdbath here. Pebble mosaics and broken crockery pieces unify and decorate a simple pedestal and basin, turning the disparate parts into an integrated whole.

Keep in mind as you look for inspiration for your garden the "unofficial motto" of Tiffany and Company Design Studios: "Nature is the best designer." It's hard to imagine a better "vision" to draw on.

Embroidered Daisy Tote

A LESS THAN PERFECT SCRAP OF EMBROIDERY ON unbleached cotton twill in a sunny daisy pattern was the starting point for this summery tote. The scrap is backed with linen and edged with a multitoned green rickrack whose colors complement the design and help to hide some marks on the edge of the fabric. The embroidered piece appears to be made from a preprinted panel — which were readily available in the first half of the twentieth century. It has the pared-down, simplified charm typical of American embroidery. Constructing the tote is really quite simple and easy.

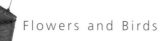

2 With a ruler and pencil, mark a 19x16-inch rectangle on the green linen. Cut it out with scissors. Use it as a pattern to cut four more pieces the same size from the green linen. Set two pieces aside for the bag lining, two pieces for the back, and the fifth will be used as the backing for the embroidered piece.

3 Cut a piece of fusible web to size and, following the directions on the package, position the fusible between two pieces of linen with the right sides of the linen facing out. With the iron, again following the directions on the package, fuse the two pieces of linen together. This will be the back of the bag.

4 Do the same with the second piece of linen and the floral embroidered fabric to make the front of the bag. Set front and back pieces aside. [photo b]

5 Assemble the lining: With the right sides facing, pin the two lining pieces together along the side seams and along the bottom edge. Machine stitch them together, allowing a $1/2$-inch seam allowance. Press all the seams to one side. To make the bottom shape, with the lining still inside out, flatten one corner so the side seam is centered and the corner forms a triangle. Measure an equal distance up each side of the triangle from the point and place pins across the intersecting line to form the base of the triangle — refer to photo c. Machine stitch across and press along that line, folding the corner under the bottom toward the center. Repeat on the other side. Pin the points of the triangles (or corners) into place along the bottom seam and tack them down, if desired. [photo c]

1 With a ruler and pencil, mark a 19x16-inch rectangle on the floral embroidered fabric, centering the design. Cut it out with scissors. [photo a]

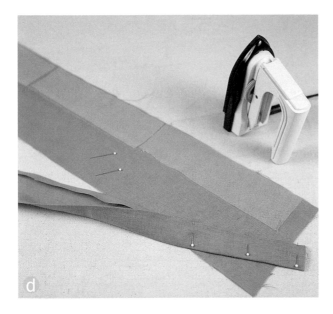

d

- Embroidered panel
- Soft lead pencil
- Clear plastic ruler
- Scissors
- 1¹/₂ yards of pale green (or other color to match panel) linen
- Pins
- Fusible web
- Household iron
- Thread to match fabric and trim
- Sewing machine
- 40 inches of 1-inch-wide multigreen (or other color to match) rickrack

6 Assemble the outer bag: With the right sides facing, pin the front and back pieces together along the sides and along the bottom edge. Machine stitch them together, allowing a ¹/₂-inch seam allowance. Press all the seams to one side. To make the bottom shape, with bag still inside out, flatten one corner so that the side seam is centered and the corner forms a triangle. Measure an equal distance up each side of the triangle from the point and place pins across the intersecting line to form the base of the triangle — refer to photo c. Machine stitch across and press along that line, folding the corner under the bottom toward the center. Repeat on the other side. Pin the points of the triangles (or corners) into place along the bottom seam and tack them down, if desired. Turn bag right side out.

7 Assemble the handles: Cut two 6x28-inch strips from the linen. Cut two 2¹/₂x26-inch strips from the fusible web, piecing the fusible if necessary. Position a strip of fusible down one side of a linen strip and fold the strip back on itself along the edge of the fusible, leaving ¹/₂ inch of linen exposed. Following the directions on the fusible package, use the iron to fuse the piece together. Fold the extra ¹/₂ inch of linen over to cover the long raw edge and press into place. Fold the handle in half again the long way. The handle will at this point measure 1¹/₄ inches wide. Pin it together along the edge and top stitch along each long edge to finish. Press. [photo d]

8 Assemble the bag: Turn and press ¹/₂ inch of fabric to the inside along the top edge of both the bag lining and the outer bag. Pin the handles into place on the inside of the outer bag, allowing 2 inches on each handle end to fall below the top edge and spacing each handle end 8 inches apart. Machine stitch the handles into place. Place the lining inside the bag with the raw edges facing each other and pin them together along the top edge. Machine stitch along the edge. Pin the rickrack into place along the top edge of the bag and machine stitch it into place. (The finished size of the bag will be 18 inches wide and 15 inches deep.) [photo e]

e

Flower Holder and Shelf

THESE SMALL METAL PIECES ARE PERFECT STARTER projects — the results are quite dramatic and easily achieved. Unlike a larger piece that has many surfaces and corners, these are easily and quickly stripped of their painted finishes, so the time and work involved are not as daunting. Frequently, larger pieces have also acquired many layers of paint. These types of small-scale metal pieces generally have a single layer, perhaps two, of paint that is easily removed. It is always something of a surprise to see what kind of surface emerges, but that is part of the fun. If you like the look of the raw metal, it will need to be protected after stripping by spraying with a clear lacquer finish — or you can finish the piece with a coat of metallic spray paint.

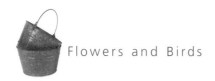

Materials

- Metal flower holder
- Metal shelf
- Old newspapers or plastic drop cloth
- Paint remover for metal
- Spray bottle
- Stripping brush
- Protective mask
- Protective eyewear
- Heavy-duty rubber gloves
- Toothbrush
- Soft rag
- Mineral spirits
- Clear spray lacquer
- Metallic spray paint

1 Spread newspaper or a plastic drop cloth over the work area. Remove the paint from the metal pieces with paint remover, following the directions on the container.

2 Scrub off the softened paint using the stripping brush. Make sure to work outside or in a well-ventilated space and wear a protective mask, eyewear, gloves, and clothing. If necessary, apply a second coat of remover. Use an old toothbrush to remove the last of the softened paint from hard-to-reach narrow crevices. Remove any residue of paint remover by wiping the piece with a rag dipped in mineral spirits. [photos a and b]

3 Once the metal is stripped, avoid letting it come in contact with water, which can cause rust to form. To protect the metal finish, spray the pieces with two coats of clear spray lacquer or a metallic spray paint. Let the lacquer or paint dry completely between each coat and after the final coat. [photos c and d]

Galvanized Metal Planters

PLANTERS OF DIFFERENT SHAPES AND SIZES MADE FROM metal have been in use for hundreds of years. Provided you can add holes for drainage, almost any hollow metal object can be recycled into a planter. Large and small metal tubs, battered buckets, old watering cans, or even an old metal wheelbarrow can make amusing and charming containers for a variety of plants. They can also be grouped together quite effectively. Best of all is that they can usually be bought for a few dollars. All of the galvanized buckets pictured here were picked up at the local dump. Here the classic no-fail color combination of purple, pink, and blue flowers is superbly set off by the silvery gray of the metal containers.

① Use the hammer and a large nail to punch many holes in the bottom of a metal tub for drainage. [photo a]

② Place a layer of broken crockery or pebbles in the bottom of the container over the drainage holes to prevent the soil from getting waterlogged and washing out. If you are not using potting mix that has water-storing granules mixed in, add some yourself to the mix. Fill the container ³/4 full with the potting mix.

③ Decide where you want to place the plants. Once you are happy with the way they look, gently release them from their plastic pots and plant them in the tubs. [photo b]

④ If the roots are very tangled and ingrown, cut them apart with a 5-way garden tool or small knife and tease them out from the root ball before planting. [photo c]

⑤ Secure the plants in place by adding more potting mix. Press down firmly on the potting mix around the plants and water thoroughly. [photo d]

Materials

- Galvanized metal tubs
- 1 large nail
- Hammer
- Broken crockery or pebbles
- Trowel
- Container-potting mix and water-storing granules
- 5-way garden tool or small knife

For each container:
- 1 geranium in bright pink

- 4–6 salvia plants in lilac and purple
- 1 *Browallia* (amethyst flower) in blue
- 1 sweet potato vine, or *Ipomoea,* in chartreuse
- 1 'wave' petunia in pale pink
- 2 fan flowers, or *Scaevola aemula,* in purple
- 1 *Evolvulus glomeratus* in blue
- 1 licorice plant in gray green

ARRANGING PLANTS IN CONTAINERS
Start in the center with the taller plants; place the shorter plants around the central bunch. Fill spaces on the edges with trailing plants. Look for trailing foliage plants like licorice plant, sweet potato vine, or vinca vine with silvery colored foliage, bright chartreuse greens, or variegated leaves that will set off the colors of your flowers. Add some flowering plants that will flow over the edge. Do not mix variegated leaves — one type per container is enough. If in doubt about what plants look good together, stick to a selective color palette — either hot colors like red, orange, and yellow or the cool blue, purple, and pink shades pictured here.

Pebble Mosaic Birdbath

NO GARDEN IS COMPLETE WITHOUT A BIRDBATH, AND THE one here makes use of recycled china pieces and robin's-egg blue pebbles to embellish the base. Bases and basins like these can be purchased separately at garden centers. As these two did not match, decorating the base was an easy way to tie the two pieces together. Save your bits of broken china or look for chipped china in pretty patterns at flea markets or thrift stores. The pebbles for this project can be easily ordered from mail-order sources or found in craft stores.

2 Use the tile nippers to cut small square or rectangular pieces from broken china, taking advantage of any repeating pattern on the china. Apply the adhesive as above and set the china pieces and small blue oblong-shaped pebbles in a ring above the first row, alternating the china and pebbles as you go. [photo b]

3 Next, set a row of the largest blue pebbles in a ring above the previous row, using the same method as above. Fill in the rest of the lower part of the base with two rings of small black pebbles, again using the same method. [photo c]

4 Use oblong-shaped blue pebbles standing on edge to fill the area along the top sloped edge of the base. As above, with the palette knife spread a $1/4$-inch layer of adhesive over a small area and stick the pebbles in place around the edge.

1 Start by sorting the blue pebbles by size and shape. For the first row of the lower part of the base, use the largest and flattest oval-shaped pebbles. Wearing gloves, mix the adhesive with water until it is fairly stiff in consistency but easily spreadable. With a palette knife, spread a $1/4$-inch layer over a small area on the lower edge of the base. Stick one ring of pebbles to the lower edge of the base. [photo a]

M a t e r i a l s

- Ceramic base and basin
- Blue river pebbles in assorted sizes and shapes
- Small black pebbles
- Containers for sorting pebbles
- Latex gloves

- Cement-based frostproof and waterproof adhesive
- Container for mixing adhesive
- Palette knife
- Tile nippers
- China pieces

5 Use the tile nippers to cut more square or rectangular pieces from the china using a different part of the pattern on the china. Apply the adhesive as above and set the china pieces and small blue oblong-shaped pebbles in a vertical row running up the center of the base, alternating the china and pebbles as you go. Repeat on the opposite side of the base. Fill in the empty areas between the two vertical rows with horizontal rows of blue pebbles, starting with the largest ones in the lower rows and graduating to smaller ones as you progress up. [photo d]

6 Optional: To give the underside of the basin an aged look, coat it with a slurry made from leftover adhesive and water. Before cleaning out the container used for mixing the adhesive, add enough water to make a soupy, sludgy mixture. Turn the basin upside down and pour the mixture over the underside of the basin. Rub the mixture into the surface. Repeat until the desired effect is achieved.

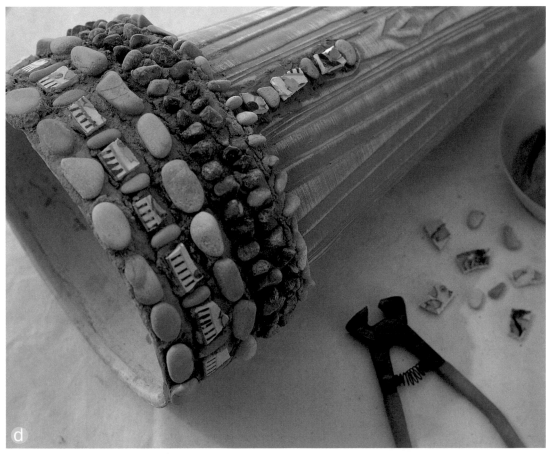

Antique Wooden Trellis

THIS WELL-WEATHERED TRELLIS FOUND AT A JUNK shop had a nicely distressed finish that was worth preserving. It's too fragile to be used in the garden, where it would be exposed to the elements, but it's perfect for a sheltered spot on the porch. Adding a mirror behind the diamond-shaped opening provides an easy trompe l'oeil effect and creates an illusion of depth. Look for elegantly shaped tall and narrow terra-cotta pots for the vinca vine — they complement the shape of the trellis and add more interest than ordinary terra-cotta pots.

1. To determine the size and shape of the mirror, place paper over the opening on the back of the trellis and trace its outline with pencil. Use a ruler to straighten the lines. Cut out a pattern and lay it on the trellis to check. Make any corrections to the pattern, if needed. Mark the front (mirror) side of the pattern. Bring the pattern to a glass and mirror store and have them cut a mirror to size.

2. Attach the mirror to the back of the trellis using clear plastic mirror holders. If needed, make spacers out of small squares of wood lath or mat board to fit between the hangers and the mirror. [photo a]

3. Fashion hangers out of the floral wire: Bend a piece of wire around the upper middle section of a terra-cotta pot until the ends meet and cross. Leaving one end long, use needle-nose pliers to twist the shorter end around the long end to make a circle and hold it in place. [photo b]

4. Take the circle off the pot and, using the pliers, continue to twist the shorter end around itself to hold the open circle in place. [photo c]

5. Bend the other, longer end of the wire in half and back on itself. Use the pliers to twist the end around itself to hold it in place and form a loop for hanging. Slide the hanger back on the pot and push it up as far as it will go. The loop should extend slightly above the rim of the pot — if not, refashion the hanger or make another one. Make two more hangers and slide them onto the other two pots. [photo c]

Materials

- Trellis
- Paper
- Pencil
- Clear plastic ruler
- Mirror cut to size of opening in trellis
- Screwdriver
- 4 clear plastic mirror hangers and screws
- Wood lath or mat board
- 3 terra-cotta pots
- 3 18-inch lengths of heavy-duty cloth-covered floral wire
- Needle-nose pliers
- Broken crockery or pebbles
- Trowel
- Container-potting mix and water-storing granules
- 5-way garden tool or small knife
- 3 vinca vine plants
- 3 small flat-head nails
- Hammer

6 Place a piece or two of broken crockery or some pebbles in the bottom of each pot over the drainage holes to prevent the soil from washing out. If you are not using potting mix that has water-storing granules mixed in, add some yourself to the mix. Fill the pots 3/4 full with the potting mix.

7 Release the vines from their pots and plant them in the terra-cotta pots. If the roots are very tangled and ingrown, cut them apart with a 5-way garden tool or small knife and tease them out from the root ball before planting. Secure the plants in place by adding more potting mix. Press down firmly on the potting mix around the plants and water thoroughly.

8 Hammer three small flat-head nails into the trellis for hanging the pots, one in the center and one on each side, staggering them if desired, as shown below. Attach the trellis to a wall or hang it in a sheltered place. Hang the terra-cotta pots on the nails. [photo d]

Rustic Hanging Planter

SMALL, UNUSUAL CONTAINERS LIKE THIS RUSTIC SEED

planter — turned into a cache for a few plants — can be a good

way to brighten up a plain wall or fence. The cheerful little

daisies and hot-colored nasturtiums complement the

faded red of the wood and the rusted metal cylinder.

Check before planting to make sure that the water

will drain out; add holes if necessary. (See step

1 of Galvanized Metal Planters on page 126

for instructions.)

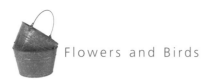

Flowers and Birds

Materials

- Corn-seed planter
- Pliers
- Screwdriver
- Broken crockery or pebbles
- Trowel
- Container-potting mix and water-storing granules
- 5-way garden tool or small knife
- Dahlberg daisy in pale yellow
- Sanvitalia
- Nasturtium mix in hot colors (reds and oranges)
- Hammer
- 1 nail

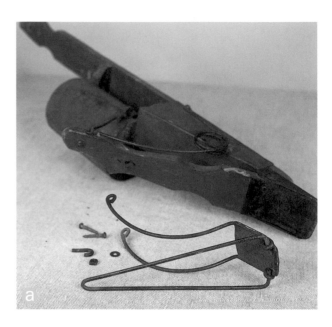

138

① Using pliers and a screwdriver, carefully remove the screws and hook holding the metal contraption to the front piece of wood. Carefully set them aside in a safe place and label them in case you want to reassemble the planter later. [photo a]

② Place a layer of broken crockery or pebbles in the bottom of the metal cylinder to prevent the soil from getting waterlogged. [photo b]

③ If you are not using potting mix that has water-storing granules mixed in, add some yourself to the mix. Fill the container ³/4 full with the potting mix.

④ Decide where you want to place the plants. Once you are happy with the way they look, gently release them from their plastic pots and plant them. If the roots are very tangled and ingrown, cut them apart with a 5-way garden tool or small knife and tease them out from the root ball before planting. Secure the plants in place by adding more potting mix. Firm the potting mix around the plants by patting down with your hands and water thoroughly. [photo c]

⑤ Hang the planter on a nail in a sunny but sheltered spot outside.

Basic Techniques

Tools

I strongly recommend investing in the three items below before starting on any of the projects in this book. Though you can do any of the projects in the book without them, they will save you hours of prep time and more than repay your investment in the long term.

- Although you can easily sand small pieces by hand, having a lightweight orbital sander will make short work of most sanding chores, especially if you are planning to do two or more furniture makeovers. Look for one that's light and easy for you to maneuver. It can save you hours of preparation time.

- I also suggest buying a cordless electric drill, which is both a power drill and a screwdriver. I found it very liberating when I finally decided to invest in one. In addition to using it for your makeovers, I guarantee that you will find almost daily use for it around the house. Look for one that's on the small side; it will be easier to handle, as the battery pack can make them awkward and heavy. Hold a few in your hand to judge which one feels the most comfortable.

- It's also a sound investment to acquire a few good-quality paintbrushes that won't lose their bristles. If you take proper care of them, you will have them forever, and you will be thankful every time you paint not to be picking out loose bristles left behind by cheap paintbrushes.

ESSENTIAL TOOL KIT

- adjustable wrench
- cordless electric drill
- craft knife
- hammer
- lead pencil
- masking tape
- metal-edge ruler
- orbital sander
- permanent marker
- pliers
- putty knife
- retractable metal tape measure
- rubber mallet
- screwdrivers, both flat-head and Phillips
- single-edge razor blades
- staple gun and staples
- wire cutters
- wood glue

ESSENTIAL PAINTING KIT

- combing tool
- cheesecloth
- household paintbrushes
- large and small disposable foam brushes
- painter's tape
- paper towels
- soft cotton rags (old white cotton T-shirts make the best rags)
- square- and round-tip artist's brushes
- stencil brush

ESSENTIAL REFINISHING KIT

- 6-in-1 painter's tool
- fine-grade sandpaper or sanding sponge
- fine-grade steel wool
- heavy-duty rubber gloves
- old toothbrushes and dental pick
- plastic scraper
- plastic stripping brush
- protective mask
- protective eyewear
- wire brush

ESSENTIAL SEWING KIT

- clear plastic gridded ruler
- cloth tape measure
- hand-sewing needles
- household iron
- glass-head straight pins
- pincushion
- rotary cutter and mat
- seam ripper or single-edge razor blades
- scissors for fabric
- scissors for paper
- soft lead pencil
- spray bottle (use for water when ironing)
- thread in white, black, and beige
- water-soluble fabric marker

ESSENTIAL CRAFT KIT

- cotton swabs
- craft glue
- craft knife
- decoupage medium
- disposable foam brushes
- glaze medium
- lead pencil/eraser
- latex gloves
- masking and white tape
- metal ruler
- nail scissors
- repositional spray adhesive
- small bottles of artist's pigment in basic colors (white, black, red, yellow, blue, green, violet, orange, raw umber, burnt sienna)
- small spray bottles
- square- and round-tip artist's brushes
- scissors

Cleaning

HOW TO CLEAN WOOD

- Fill a container with warm water and add a small amount of a mild dish-washing detergent (like Ivory). Dip a soft, clean rag in the water, wring out well, and wipe the wood with the damp rag.
- Do not soak the wood or let the water sit on it. Wipe it dry with clean rags or paper towels.

HOW TO CLEAN WICKER

- Fill a container with warm water and add a cleaning agent (like Soilex) or, if it's just surface dirt, a small amount of a mild dishwashing detergent (like Ivory). Dip a soft, clean sponge in the water and wipe the wicker with the damp sponge.
- Use an old toothbrush to clean in the corners and crevices that are hard to reach with the sponge.
- Rinse well and let the wicker dry outdoors in the sun.
- Rub a small amount of linseed oil into the surface of natural unpainted wicker to restore its luster.

HOW TO REMOVE LIGHT RUST ON IRON OR STEEL

- Apply naval jelly to the surface. Leave on for 5 to 20 minutes. Rinse off with water. Repeat if any rust remains. You can also rub the surface lightly with a fine-grade steel wool pad over the naval jelly.
- Alternatively, for very light rust, rub the surface with a steel wool pad dipped in vegetable oil.
- Use these techniques only on steel or iron. Do not use on aluminum or chrome.

HOW TO REMOVE LIGHT STAINS ON CHROME-PLATED TUBULAR STEEL AND ALUMINUM

- Use a rubbing compound formulated for chrome/aluminum.
- Apply a light coat of silicone furniture polish to protect the finish.

HOW TO REMOVE LIGHT STAINS ON MARBLE

• Rub light stains with toothpaste and a clean rag using lots of elbow grease.
• Wipe clean with a damp rag or paper towel. Dry with a clean rag or paper towel.

HOW TO POLISH SMALL METAL FITTINGS

• Use a small amount of toothpaste and an old toothbrush to give a quick polish to small metal fittings like knobs and hinges.
• Wipe clean with a damp rag or rinse in water and dry.

HOW TO REMOVE RUST STAINS ON FABRIC

• Dip half a lemon in salt. Rub it directly on the stain and let it sit for a few minutes.
• Stretch the fabric over the top of any heat-resistant (metal or tempered-glass) bowl.
• Pour boiling water through the fabric until the stain is out.

HOW TO REMOVE OLD TAPE OR STICKERS ON GLASS

• Rub the surface of the sticker or tape with a cloth dampened with white vinegar.
• Or rub a small amount of peanut butter into the sticker until it dislodges.
• Rinse with soapy water.
• Nail polish remover, turpentine, and prewash spray can also be effective in loosening the glue on stickers.

HOW TO CLEAN GLASS OR GLASSWARE

• Fill a spray bottle with water to which you have added a small amount of ammonia and spray the solution on the surface of the glass.
• Dry and polish the glass with wadded-up newspapers.
• Wash glassware in warm, soapy water, adding a small amount of white vinegar to the rinse water.
• If glassware remains cloudy, try soaking it overnight in a bowl of water to which you have added a denture-cleaning tablet.

R e p a i r i n g

HOW TO TIGHTEN JOINTS ON WOODEN FURNITURE

- Use a shim to tighten rectangular joints. This works especially well for the stretchers that fit in the legs of chairs and tables, which frequently become loose through hard use.
- Make a shim out of a small scrap of hardwood. It can be of even thickness or slightly tapered, but it should be as wide as the hole.
- Apply glue to the hole and drive the shim into place. Apply more glue and reassemble the joint. Wipe any excess glue off with a damp rag.
- Use cloth strips for round or square joints. Cut cloth (from an old sheet or shirt) into strips. The strips should be narrower than the end of the part you're inserting.
- Place the strips over the end of the part in the form of an X. Trim the strips on the sides so they are about two thirds of the depth of the joint — the cloth will stretch when the pieces are joined.
- Apply glue to the hole and reassemble the joint. Trim any cloth protruding after the joint is assembled with a razor blade and wipe any excess glue off with a damp rag.

HOW TO FILL SMALL CRACKS, SURFACE DENTS, HOLES, AND OTHER SURFACE BLEMISHES ON WOODEN PIECES

- Working on a clean surface, use a putty knife to apply a lightweight spackling paste or wood putty over any cracks or other dents. Deeper holes might need more than one application of the paste.
- Push the paste down into the cracks with the putty knife. Draw a damp knife across the surface, smoothing the excess paste as you go. Let the putty dry until it is hard.
- The paste type of filler does not usually require sanding, but if necessary, sand the surface lightly with fine-grade sandpaper.

Getting Started

Careful surface preparation will give you the best results. Frequently you can paint over the original finish if you take the time to prepare the surface carefully.

HOW TO PREPARE WOODEN PIECES FOR PAINTING OR REFINISHING

- Use a power sander or sandpaper to sand any previously painted surface to provide a smooth, nonglossy, paintable surface (be sure to wear a protective mask).
- If the finish or paint is too thick, badly cracked, sticky, or uneven, it can be removed with paint remover, following the directions on the container. If you decide to remove the old paint or finish entirely, sand the piece when you are done.
- Remove sanding dust with a soft rag before proceeding to paint or refinish.

HOW TO PREPARE METAL PIECES FOR PAINTING OR RESURFACING

- Use a wire brush or sander to remove any loose, flaking metal or paint to provide a smooth, paintable surface.
- If there are too many layers of paint to sand, they can be removed with a paint remover especially formulated for metal, following the directions on the container.
- If the piece is very rusty, apply a product like Rust-Oleum Rust Reformer, which bonds with the metal to form a smooth, paintable surface.

Refinishing

HOW TO REMOVE OLD PAINT OR MULTIPLE FINISHES FROM WOOD, METAL, OR WICKER FURNITURE

- Use a paint remover specifically formulated for your surface. There are removers for use on either metal or wood surfaces. Work outside where possible or in a well-ventilated work space.

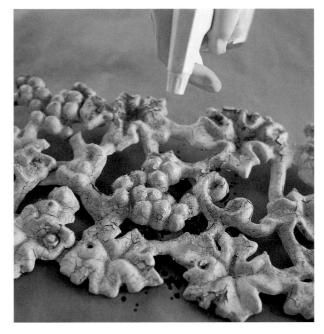

- Wear heavy-duty rubber gloves and a protective mask. Apply the remover liberally with an old paintbrush or spray bottle. Let the remover stand for 15 to 20 minutes until the finish is softened and the surface appears crinkly. Don't let the remover dry out.

- Remove the loosened paint or finish by scraping it with a plastic scraper, 6-in-1 painter's tool, rounded-edge putty knife, or a plastic stripping brush. Which tool you use depends on the type of surface involved.

- Wipe off as much of the remaining finish as possible using crumpled paper towels. Dip a pad of fine-grade steel wool in the solvent recommended (generally mineral spirits) on the container and scrub the surface for a final cleaning. Wipe the surface dry with a clean rag.
- For wicker, keep the surface wet by applying the remover with a spray bottle. Use a plastic stripping brush to remove the finish. Use a toothbrush (or cut down an old paintbrush) dipped in mineral spirits or the solvent recommended on the paint remover container to finish cleaning the surface.

HOW TO VARNISH STRIPPED AND UNPAINTED WOOD SURFACES

- Use a protective, penetrating oil finish (like Formby's Tung Oil Finish in low gloss) for a natural, classic look. This type of finish penetrates the wood and dries clear, allowing the natural beauty of the wood to shine.
- After preparing the surface, rub a small amount of tung oil into the wood using a soft, clean rag. Allow it to dry and buff it with a fine-grade steel wool pad. Wipe it down with a clean rag and repeat until you have achieved the desired finish, then let it dry completely.

HOW TO REMOVE HEAVY RUST ON IRON OR STEEL FURNITURE

- Remove heavy rust by using a power drill with a wire brush attachment. Grind as much of the loose rust and corrosion off the surface as you can.
- Use a wire brush to clean in the corners and crevices that are hard to reach with the drill. Wear heavy-duty gloves, a protective mask, and plastic goggles.

HOW TO ACHIEVE A BRUSHED FINISH ON STRIPPED STEEL FURNITURE

- For an attractive brushed-metal finish, attach a medium wire brush to a power drill and work slowly and evenly across the surface to smooth and polish it.
- Keep the drill moving to achieve an overall brushed-satin finish.
- The surface will need to be protected, so finish it with a coat or two of clear satin spray lacquer.

HOW TO MAINTAIN A RUSTED SURFACE ON METAL

• To maintain the look of rusted metal, first brush the surface with a wire brush to remove loose particles, then rub the piece with boiled linseed oil and let it soak in overnight.

• Wipe off the excess linseed oil and protect the surface with a final spray of clear matte acrylic sealer from a craft store.

P a i n t i n g

HOW TO PREPARE WOOD FOR PAINTING

• Sand the piece with a power sander or by hand with sandpaper or a sanding sponge.

• Remove the dust with a rag or a brush and wipe the surface down with a damp paper towel. Let it dry thoroughly.

HOW TO PRIME WOOD BEFORE PAINTING

• If you need to prime the surface, I recommend using an acrylic primer like Benjamin Moore Fresh Start, which adheres well to a variety of surfaces, is quick drying, and cleans up with water.

• Apply one coat and let it dry thoroughly. Sand the surface lightly and remove the dust before proceeding.

HOW TO PRIME METAL BEFORE PAINTING

• Metal can be primed, as above for wood, with an acrylic primer.

• If the piece is very rusty, treat it first with Rust-Oleum Rust Reformer, a product that chemically converts rust into a smooth, paintable surface. There's no need to sand all the way down to the bare metal; just remove as much of the rust as possible. Apply the Rust Reformer as directed on the package.

• For further protection, follow this by priming with a rust-preventive metal-specific primer.

HOW TO PAINT WITH WATER-BASED PAINT

- For outdoor pieces, look for either a satin-finish paint like Benjamin Moore MoorGlo or MoorGard (which have a slight sheen) or an enamel finish like Benjamin Moore Impervex (which has a high-gloss finish).
- Two coats of paint are best, but sometimes one will do. Let the first coat dry, then sand the surface lightly and remove the dust before applying the second coat. Let pieces dry thoroughly before using them.

AGE NEW PAINT

- New paint can be given a vintage look by applying a transparent glaze to the surface after the paint has dried. Add a small amount of raw umber to some water or glaze medium and lightly brush the mixture onto the painted item.
- If it still looks too new once the glaze dries, repeat the procedure or try lightly washing the piece with water.

Setting Up Your Work Space

THINGS TO HAVE ON HAND BEFORE STARTING

- Paper towels
- Clean rags
- Ziploc bags in assorted sizes
- Large plastic trash bags (tape or hang one up nearby)
- Rubber gloves
- Plastic goggles
- Protective mask and/or respirator
- Appropriate solvent for paint or refinisher
- Assorted containers and buckets (save your larger metal coffee or food cans; they make good containers for solvents, paint, mixing, etc.)

GETTING READY TO REFINISH

- It's best to work outdoors, as stripping is messy and smelly. If that is not possible, a basement or garage, with proper ventilation, is another choice.
- Spread a heavy-duty drop cloth on the floor or work surface and layer with newspapers or a plastic drop cloth.
- Use a fan to increase ventilation, and open all doors and windows.
- Wear heavy-duty rubber gloves, safety glasses, and a respirator or a protective mask.
- Have paper towels handy.

GETTING READY TO PAINT

- Painting is messy and sloppy, so work a safe distance from walls and furniture.
- Spread a heavy-duty drop cloth on the floor or work surface, or layer the work area with newspapers.
- Open doors and windows if you are working inside.
- If you are working outside, be sure to paint only when it is not windy or very humid.
- Have a bucket of water or solvent handy for brush cleanup.
- If you have to stop before you are finished, place the brush (or roller) in a plastic bread bag or other thin plastic bag, squeeze out the air, and tie it firmly closed around the handle.

• If you can't resume painting in a few hours, place the whole wrapped brush (or roller) in a large Ziploc bag and pop it in the freezer. It will stay wet indefinitely.

GETTING READY TO SPRAY PAINT

• Outdoors is best, but spray painting can be done indoors in a very well ventilated area.
• Open all the windows and doors and wear a respirator or protective mask.
• Prepare a large work area, as for painting. For smaller objects, you can construct a mini spray booth by cutting the top and one side off a smallish cardboard box.
• The best way to ensure even coverage is to spray many light coats. Move the can in a slow, even movement across the object being sprayed. Don't stop when you get to the edge but continue slightly over the sides and then go back in the other direction. Continue until the object is evenly coated with paint.

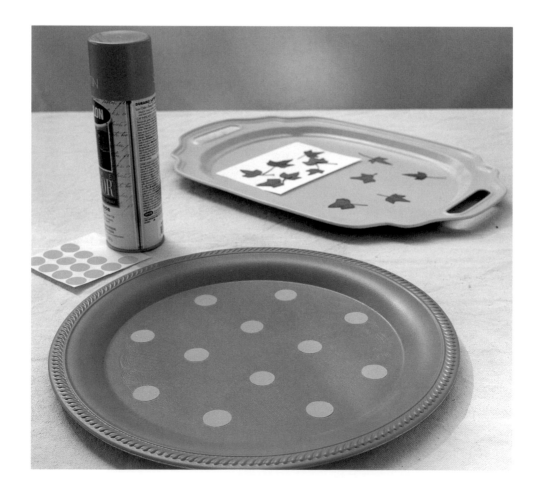

Resources

FABRICS, TRIMS, AND SEWING SUPPLIES

Calico Corners
203 Gale Lane
Kenner Square, PA 19348
800-213-6366
www.calicocorners.com
Discount top quality fabrics

Fairfield Processing
www.poly-fil.com
Soft Touch pillow inserts, low-loft polyester batting

Jo-Ann Fabric
1-888-739-4120
www.joann.com
Fabrics, trims, upholstery, and sewing supplies

Laura Ashley for Kravet
800-648-4686
www.kravet.com
Wide range of home decorating fabrics, including a selection of Sunbrella outdoor fabrics

Mokuba
55 West 38th Street
New York, NY 10018
212-869-8900
212-869-8970 fax
Outstanding ribbons, passementerie, and lace

Oilcloth International
134 North Avenue 61, Building #101
Los Angeles, CA 90042
323-344-3967
323-344-0409 fax
www.oilcloth.com
Patterned oilcloth

Rose Brand
75 Ninth Ave
New York, NY 10011
212-242-7565
www.rosebrand.com
Canvas, muslin, and outdoor fabrics

Rosen & Chadick
246 West 40th Street
New York, NY
212-869-0136
Linen and cotton basics

CRAFT, PAINT, AND OTHER SUPPLIES

Anna Griffin
733 Lambert Drive
Atlanta, GA 31324
404-817-8170
www.annagriffin.com
Decorative papers and die-cuts, fine invitations and writing papers

Benjamin Moore
51 Chestnut Ridge Road
Montvale, NJ 07645
800-344-0400
www.benjaminmoore.com
Manufacturer of exterior and interior paint

Dick Blick Art Materials
P.O. Box 1267
Galesburg, Il 61402
800-828-4548
www.dickblick.com
Mosaic and art supplies

Michael's Crafts
800-642-4235
www.michaels.com
Craft and art supplies

Plaid
P.O. Box 7600
Norcross, GA 30091
800-842-4197
www.plaidonline.com
Manufacturer of craft and home decor products

HARDWARE, LUMBER, AND TOOLS

Dykes Lumber Company
1899 Park Avenue
Weehawken, NJ 07087
201-867-0391
201-867-1674 fax
www.dykeslumber.com
The largest stock of moldings in the East

Home Depot
800-353-3199
www.homedepot.com

Lowe's
800-445-6937
www.lowes.com

REFERENCE BOOKS

Creative Garden Mosaics
Jill Mackay
Lark Books/Sterling Publishing, New York
Techniques, projects, and step-by-step instructions for outdoor mosaics

The Complete Book of Paint
David Carter
Sterling Publishing, New York

The Complete Guide to Repairing & Restoring Furniture
William J. Cook
Anness Publishing, London
Step-by-step guide to basic furniture repairs and restoration

Pebble Mosaics
Deborah Schneebeli-Morrell and Gloria Nicol
Firefly Books
Projects and step-by-step instructions for pebble mosaics

Simply Pillows
Sunset Books, Menlo Park, CA
Basics of making decorative and accent pillows with comprehensive instructions and step-by-step illustrations

Simply Upholstery
Sunset Books, Menlo Park, CA
Upholstery basics with detailed step-by-step illustrations and instructions

Index